C Companion ™

Sales Meeting Companion™

Authored by   **Dave Skrobot**
and   **Mike Rolland**

Companion ™

Printed in Canada

Note for Librarians: a cataloguing record for this book that includes Dewey Classification and US Library of Congress numbers is available from the National Library of Canada. The complete cataloguing record can be obtained from the National Library's online database at: www.nlc-bnc.ca/amicus/index-e.html
ISBN 1-4120-2855-8

10   9   8   7   6   5   4

SALES MEETING COMPANION™ MISSION STATEMENT

"To educate Managers of Sales Teams by giving them the tools and techniques for facilitating more productive Sales Meetings in order to better motivate and inform their employees."

TEAMS

T oolbook to

E ducate

A nd

M otivate

S ales staff

Edited by
Eva Marie Valdes

FOREWORD

Managers of Sales Teams in North America are overwhelmed with work. How then are they to come up with new, fresh and insightful information to impart to their staff on a regular basis? This observed dilemma is the genesis behind the creation of Sales Meeting Companion.

Dave Skrobot is a professional customer service and sales trainer who has travelled North America presenting his training material to Managers and employees alike. This training material has been gathered by interviewing and working with some of the most successful Managers in the US and Canada. His articles on Customer Service and improving employee performance have been showcased in newspapers and magazines throughout the continent. Now he has combined the best material and collaborated with a proven winner in co-author Mike Rolland.

Mike Rolland is presently Manager of a large sales and service team. Mike's near 25 years of Managing people at both the regional and national levels have garnered him respect and admiration of employees and co-workers alike. His experience stretches from working with sales teams in 3 continents and 5 countries across the globe. That managerial know-how has been highlighted and illustrated in this 26 chapter compendium of sales and service do's and don'ts .

CONTENTS

Part I
Storybook

Part II
Lessonbook

Part III
Toolbook

Part I
STORYBOOK

Part II
LESSONBOOK

Part III
TOOLBOOK

This symbol at the end of a chapter in Part II Lesson-book, refers to a corresponding entry in Part III, the Toolbook.

The Toolbook Reference Library.
When you see this symbol in the text, you can find an expanded explanation on the topic in Part III of this book. Many of the toolbook entries will provide you material you can photocopy and use for your meeting to encourage staff participation and help motivate them. Feel free to use the toolbook as a hand-out that you can copy and pass out to your staff or check the www.companionlearning.com web site for updates on providing material for you or your staff.

We welcome readers to comment and submit any ideas to improve customer service, increase client retention or accelerate sales. Contact the authors at salesmc@telus.net
Best ideas submission will win a Free trip to the next **Companion Rocky Mountain Summit** Managers meetings held in the beautiful Canadian Rockies.

Thanks for your interest in Sales Meeting Companion, be sure to check the web site for the next volume in the Companion series.

Web Help
Visit our web site: www.companionlearning.com

PART I
STORYBOOK

Many managers and, consequently, employees suffer from an all-too-common condition we like to call "Bad Sales Meetings". This generally results from managers who find themselves unable to come up with new, fresh and interesting material to introduce or review with staff. No easy task, we're certain you'll agree! This is why there is such a need for Sales Meeting Companion. In this book we will offer up helpful topics, which the new - or experienced - manager can utilize to create and articulate sales meetings with real impact. This book will cover many facets of customer service, teaching you how to improve sales performance with an end to increasing customer retention.

Many employees in today's work force are highly educated and need constant stimulation and reinforcement in order to realize optimum job performance. If they are subjected to the same old repetitive content in meetings they will feel they are not coming away with information that is useful in their jobs.

During these meetings some employees may feel that "instead of talking about selling, I could have been out there selling". Some others find that the information they receive may not be relevant to them in their respective situations.

Having been involved in numerous "dead end meetings" and "get- nowhere seminars", we felt there was a calling for a handbook like this one which would give you the tools you require to run successful meetings with your staff.

As a trainer I would teach Automobile Dealership employees indispensable methods to attract customers and convert them into long-term clients. Regardless of a generalized reputation the retail automotive industry may have, it is still one of the most dynamic competitive sales environments around. As in all businesses there will always be some operators representing the bottom-of-the-barrel, but by and large most of these "bad apples" have gone out to compost. This is due to, among other things, increased pressures imposed by the manufacturer. I know of no other industry that spends as much money, time, and training on customer satisfaction than the car business.

Consequently the industry has changed for the better, increasingly seeking and attracting some of the best service-minded personnel available to retail. Don't get me wrong, I realize that much of the responsibility for this heightened interest in customer service has been prompted by increased competition among, and proliferation of, new vehicles getting to market every year. (The number of vehicle choices available to the consumer has literally *tripled* in the last 15 years.) However, this increased competition puts even more pressure on dealership personnel to provide constantly improving customer service. The stiffer the competition in any business, the greater the need for top quality meetings. Let's take a look at two types of meetings.

Surprise Meetings vs. Regular Meetings

Some companies conduct scheduled weekly or bi-weekly meetings wherein they meet for 1 - 2 and sometimes 3 hours. Still other organizations might call an unscheduled, or surprise, meeting every month or two. The latter type is sure to cause more anxiety than the former amongst staff.

Picture it. A surprise meeting is called and immediately employees are on edge, possibly even alarmed. Why does this happen? Well, it's easy to figure out, an unscheduled meeting can only mean bad news! Someone's job is on the line or layoffs are being announced or perhaps even a milder concern surfaces - a reprimand is coming our way! The bottom line is that it is human nature for people to replace an absence of information with a negative, and if they don't know *why* the surprise meeting is called, they will likely assume the worst. It is normal behavior to assume the worst..

It reminds me of a situation I found myself in when I was a grade-school student in Northern Alberta. One day a fellow classmate informed me that the principal was looking for me. I was immediately alarmed, and began pondering all sorts of unconstructive predicaments I had gotten myself into of late which were possible reasons for the summons. With sweaty palms, and fearing the worst, I entered the principal's office where I was relieved and overjoyed to learn I was actually being commended for having helped one of the younger children in the school during a difficult time.

So how does this relate to sales meetings? Employees do not react any differently than I did in the situation I have just described. If it's a regular meeting – same time, same place - that's fine. If it's a surprise meeting there is a chance the employees are going to think: "What have we done now?" I used to get this often when I would put on Technician meetings in dealership service departments. Normally technicians weren't involved much in regular meetings so when a "trainer" from parts unknown arrived to speak with them, the suppositions began flying: "He's been sent to find out what is wrong with our operation and make some changes - to our *staffing or processing or pay systems – something is wrong.*" We all know that it is human nature to resist change like we resist a tax audit and the fear these technicians felt was completely normal.

Knowing of the existence of this fear and anxiety, when I met with the staff I would dispense with the usual meeting-openers - prolonged introductions and such - and instead I would ask them: "What do you think is the biggest reason I am *not* hired to work in a store like this?" I would get some predictable responses like, "You're too expensive". Then I would offer the real reason: "In all seriousness, the biggest reason I am not hired in a store like yours is that after pitching my ideas, concepts/ manuals/ training programs, the owner would typically tell me, 'Well, it seems like you know this business well, and I like how you present your ideas, but I'm not too sure that my present employees are worth the time and money it would take to implement your systems'". As a salesperson whose job it is to convince him that my course is of great value to his business, I would always find it difficult to counter that objection. So, in the situations where I was not hired to train, the number one reason was because the manager did not want to invest in the people he currently had. Obviously then, when I am hired to train I can tell the staff that their manager *does* want to invest in them.

I would use this example to ease the negative pressure on the group by enlightening them as to the reason for this particular story. No matter where the employees of the dealership came from, or how long they have been on the job, they *can* learn and grow within their area of expertise, as individuals and as a team. No matter what the sum total of a group's experience or past performance, there is always room for improvement and no dealership's staff is unworthy of the time and money it takes to realize such improvement. I feel it is of utmost importance to ensure any group I am meeting with that *they are worth it*. This immediately eases their anxiety, and gives them some positive reinforcement, which is a nice surprise, considering their mood on entering the surprise meeting!

People would rather be associated with a winner than a loser any day of the week. The car business has certainly been winning in the last few years. We have just come off some of the best years ever in our industry - in fact, from 1995 until Sept. 11, 2001, the best 5 years in automotive sales history. And with the best years in the business comes some of the best training and programs and materials that money can buy. Consider this: When the government talks about how well the economy is doing -what statistics do you suppose they look at? Usually three major ones: retail sales, new home starts, and new car sales.

I don't think many can argue that the construction and transportation businesses are the two biggest industries in the world. The construction business, although massive, is quite fragmented all over the world. There are regional homebuilders unique to every city and these are generally split up into categories of high end and middle-income builders. Mega construction companies can build high rises and shopping malls, but by and large, construction companies too are regional, unlike the Fords, the General Motors, the Hondas and Toyotas of this world. Honda, for example, built over 6 million engines in 1991. These 4 companies are worldwide in scale and actually possess the capacity to impact the economy. Salespeople need to know they are part of a large and important industry after all Sales is by far the biggest occupation of people all over the globe.

Sometimes during sales meetings, managers can get so over-zealous about budgets and quotas that they can actually de-motivate their employees without even knowing it. How can this be? Simple. As salespeople we can all remember months that were less than stellar performance-wise. Let's face it, some months we just plain sucked! Picture how humiliating it feels as a salesperson being low man/woman on the totem pole in front of your peers. This picture gets worse when you sit in a meeting listening to the manager re-count this unsatisfactory performance, rather than spending the time to motivate you to do better in the future.

The distraught salesperson walks out of the meeting head held low, feeling that he doesn't want to be humiliated again next week - so he goes out and tries to sell from desperation. He/she is no longer selling from strategy or from positive motivation, and may in fact be taking a large step toward an even less satisfactory performance in future.

"WE ARE GOING TO HAVE A MEETING!"

There are two types of people in the business world today - those who like meetings and those who do not.

What type are you?

Why?

Type I

Some people like meetings because it gives them time to hide from their real job. Some others like them because they like the sound of their own voice and it gives them a platform to grandstand; others because they find meetings informative, motivating and beneficial to their role at work. What percentage do you think fall into the latter category?

Type II

Some people dislike meetings because they fear them – they fear they will be picked on as a poor performer or they are unable to answer a direct question in front of others. Some dislike meetings because they feel they are put down publicly, or because the meetings they regularly attend are, to them, a waste of time.

Most people do not like meetings because they would rather be spending their meeting time somewhere else doing something else, and for a variety of reasons:

-   the manager holding the meeting is boring
-   the manager holding the meeting is a poor presenter
-   the manager holding the meeting always hands out complaints about poor performance
-   not sure what the purpose of the meeting is – didn't get anything out of the previous meetings
-   subject matter does not involve or benefit them
-   they genuinely believe their time is too valuable and they *do* have better things to do

FOR MANAGERS, THERE ARE REALLY ONLY TWO REASONS FOR HOLDING A MEETING:

1) To inform
2) To motivate

That's it, that's all!

That doesn't mean you only have two topics, but your staff should come out of the meeting feeling good, believing that their input was well received and will be taken into consideration for future improvements and changes. They should feel recognized as a group - a solid team - and they should be more informed about their business and the direction in which the company is heading, as well as its progress to date. AND - they should understand their role in the program(s) you have announced and the benefits to them in achieving the goals set out.

That covers the *raison d'etre* of a meeting.

WHY ARE THERE SO MANY POOR BUSINESS MEETINGS? LET'S TAKE A LOOK AT TWO GENERAL TYPES OF MEETINGS:

1) **THE REGULAR (DAILY, WEEKLY OR MONTHLY) MEETING**
2) **THE SPECIAL MEETING – CALLED TO INTRODUCE A NEW PRODUCT OR NEW POLICIES OR COMPANY STRUCTURE**

THE REGULAR MEETING

How many regular meetings have you been to where you took away nothing? As you walked out through the door you said in your mind, "That was a waste of time." Or you later found yourself in a group of peers discussing the general consensus of the meeting which was "Obviously nothing is going to change" or "I've got more important things to do than sit through that !@#*".

Well look in the mirror now that YOU are the manager and you are running these meetings. Has anything changed since you were in the group at the coffee pot complaining about the 'waste of time' meetings? Do you motivate your staff? Do you inform them? Or are you carrying on the grand old tradition of "THE REGULAR MEETING" !!! Did you forget all those times when, as an employee, you swore you would handle things better than your manager did, given the opportunity! It's easy to criticize, but perhaps now that you are a manager you have found yourself doing those very things that make for a poor, non-productive meeting. You have become that manager!

Put the effort in (preparation) to make these regular meetings a little special. Change the routine a little, keeping enough structure for the basis of the meetings, but spicing them up by doing new things. Invite guest speakers – yes, even to your little regular meetings. Bring in someone from another department to say a few words or someone from outside your company. Ensure they are aware of your meeting goals and company objectives so that they can use the right buzzwords or acronyms. Have them mention the name or names of one or two of your team members as recognition for achievements. A little praise goes a long way, especially when it comes from an accredited outside source.

Do not let your regular meetings become just a regular whining session. The only thing that should be 'regular' is the frequency of the meeting, not the content. Let me illustrate this with an example of one of my regular meetings. Years ago, I held a 'regular' meeting that shocked the members of my team - got their attention in a big way and left a lasting impression.

We would have meetings at lunchtime. Lunch was brought in and while we were eating there was general chit-chat about a variety of things, the usual stuff. Then when the food was gone I would start the formal part of the meeting. We had reached a point where the only 'new' concerns were rehashed complaints about things that various team members either did or didn't do to the annoyance of the rest of the team. My hands were tied in as much as I obviously did not possess the power to alter the bad habits of my staff, nor did I have the time to micro-supervise their every interaction. So instead I decided that a radical approach to the problem was needed. Shock treatment!

I prepared the meeting room for lunch, except I removed the lunch table. I arranged the chairs in a circle and put the food on a clean cloth – *on the floor!* When my staff arrived for the meeting, the first person in the room made a quick observation and ran out to warn the others – they'd better get there quickly and be ready for something heavy!

Everyone came in and a few smart remarks were made to my obvious disapproval. I responded only with silence. Very quickly the amusement of the people in the room diminished as my demeanor signaled a serious tone. I invited the employees to take their food and eat, informing them that I would not be joining them in the meal today as I had some serious matters to discuss with them. I stood outside the circle of chairs and flicked through my papers while they ate, in silence, their faces down-turned.

When they finished eating I started the meeting by moving to the center of the circle and advising them that this would not be a normal meeting and that they should appreciate I expected no interruptions to my presentation. Nobody could look me in the eye. They all knew we had reached the final straw about something by the seriousness of the mood, but they were not sure what it was. I explained that we had reached a turning point and that some behavioral changes needed to occur, either of their own volition or as a result of my introducing penalties for non-compliance. I reviewed the list of concerns and then laid down the law, as I saw it, from this point on. I made everyone aware that they should be ashamed of the petty whining and complaining that were all too prevalent in the current work atmosphere. I dwelt heavily on this subject, so there could be no mistake amongst the staff that this situation had gotten out of control. They all agreed there was a need for change.

Then I spoke about how good it could be if we worked in harmony, as one team rather than several little cliques, each with its own agenda. In order to soften things up after the rough beginning I then went around the circle and spoke of some of the personal characteristics of each person in turn, mentioning something I knew about every attendee that I appreciated on a personal level. I emphasized the fact that in our own way we each bring some unique characteristics to the team, and that only in working as a team will we be sure to avoid a negative work atmosphere and future meetings such as the one that had been necessitated today.

There were a lot of silent, shamed faces in the room when I finished. I left in silence and walked away. Within minutes, one at a time, people came to me and said 'we needed that' or, 'that was the best meeting we ever had' – things to that effect. I was drained but felt satisfied that we had gotten things in the open and had laid out a viable plan to improve our situation.

What took place in that meeting? After all, it was a 'regular' meeting. I'll summarize for you. Although the time, location and participants were the same, everything else was different. I shocked the staff into attention by removing the table and removing myself from the group by not joining them in the meal. Then I broke the circle and became uncomfortably close to each one of them by being in their face, in the middle of the circle. They had no choice but to look at my face, where they saw seriousness and disappointment. I took them further down by listing my concerns and identifying the individuals who were causing grief or otherwise perpetuating a negative atmosphere within the workplace. Then I softened them by making a personal statement about each of them. Lastly I gave them a picture of what things could be like and what would happen if the appropriate changes were forthcoming. By that time they were all ready and willing to acknowledge the painful truth about their childish behavior and take steps to eradicate it.

It worked. Within the hour there were visible signs of 'bridge-building' and other improvements. Before the next 'regular' meeting, when I put out the notice confirming the next get-together, one of my staff members sheepishly asked if there would be a table at the lunch meeting! We reached the point where we could laugh about it, because the need for change had existed and the requisite changes had been forthcoming.

The lesson here is: Don't let regular meetings become just a scheduled get-together. If you inherit a bad situation take the opportunity to resolve outstanding issues. Take a radical approach if you need to. Just don't allow an atmosphere to exist wherein contempt is bred - and allowed to thrive - through familiarity.

THE SPECIAL MEETING

Whether you are planning a special meeting for your regular group or for a larger group, the rules of readiness are the same. Preparation is key, especially in relation to your knowledge of the subject material. Know it better than you need to - much better. Know your audience and the markets in which they work.

The following information about preparation should not need to be mentioned. However even in large well organized companies there are far too many meetings put together that are not well prepared and as a result the distractions of equipment failures or missing material make for very unprofessional meetings put on by otherwise knowledgeable managers. Don't be one of them.

Most of us do not have an entourage of people who are standing by, ready to take care of the setup and deal with minor glitches when they arise. Again, the answer is to be prepared. If you are traveling to a location away from your regular office, take a personal interest in the meeting room arrangements. Arriving at the meeting room half an hour before the start will not do. All too often the layout will be different to that which you were expecting and not suit the style of your presentation. Most hotels and conference centers will work with you to view the room layout the evening prior to the meeting. Even if that room is in use the evening before they will work with you to find a time period that will allow you to confirm that the layout and amenities are suitable to your needs.

It is a good idea to enlist the assistance of a staff member so you can delegate some of the preparation work, involving them enough that they are able to serve as another pair of ears and eyes for you. They can help with the setup and spot potential difficulties before they arise. They can also attend to nagging details, such as locating washrooms, and planning breaks to coincide with refreshment service.

Check to ensure that the A/V (audio visual) equipment is what you ordered and that it works the way you want it to. Find out where the lighting controls are and experiment with different settings.

Have an assistant work everything for you in rehearsal so they are experienced with your needs during the actual meeting. Check the performance of the audio system. Too often speakers perform a sound check in an empty room and then, for the meeting, the sound volume is much too low. Bodies absorb sound waves, account for this when setting the volume. Avoid the classic, unprofessional 'check, check, 1-2-3, testing—can you hear me at the back?' when you go to the microphone at the start of your presentation - the hallmark of an unprepared amateur.

Have you ever had your luggage lost by an airline, or heard of it happening to an acquaintance? Yes, it happens all too frequently – but what can we learn from it? Carry a back-up plan. Have your assistant carry a second back-up. Don't learn this the hard way. These days it is easy to carry additional disc copies of a Power-Point presentation. Even if you have your own laptop and projector equipment, check ahead of time that the hotel has a loaner or rental available should you need it. If you are renting equipment that will be delivered to the room make sure you and your assistant are familiar with it and know how to repair minor difficulties, like switching to the back-up bulb of an overhead projector.

When the meeting room is booked in advance, use this little tip to ensure access to the room in good time. Advise the hotel that your meeting starts at 9:30 am and runs until noon, at which time you would like lunch served. Tell them you need the room set up at 7:00 am and you will need access at that time. In most cases they will set the room up the night before so you can have the opportunity to do your checks and A/V tests. Make sure they understand the time on the notice board in the lobby reads the correct meeting times: 9:30 am start - not 7:00 am. Too often the hotel will just look up the times the room is booked for and copy those times on their notice boards. That error happens every day in hotels in every city. Avoid it by being prepared.

Be as prepared as you possibly can for eventualities and as familiar as you can be with your meeting room surroundings. This will allow you to use any nervous energy before the meeting to boost your confidence instead of diverting it to worry about setup and other issues.

If your meeting is on home turf then the references to working with hotels will not apply, but the preparation and use of an assistant will. You still need a back up plan for the A/V material.

LEADERSHIP

You know what you want for your department and your business - to be the leader in your field, the best team, the highest achievers and the biggest earners with loyal, satisfied team members. So why is this so difficult to achieve? Is it because you do not have what it takes? Technically you know the job, you know the product and you know your customers, but you may have a weak team. You don't produce like other departments or competing companies. Maybe you are just not one of those managers with the ability to motivate; you are not the flamboyant type and you can't be something you're not, right?

WELL ... don't look for excuses, look for improvements. If performance in your area of responsibility needs improving, here is the good news: the worse it is, the more potential you have for growth and success! Study the information in this book, practice what you learn, and you will improve beyond what you thought possible.

Is it easy? NO.
Is it possible? YES.
Can I do it? If you really want to.

This book is not about miracles, it is about training. In fact, it is designed to be used by you as exactly that: a training manual.

In order to achieve the maximum benefits from this training program, you will be required to do your part by putting into practice the four characteristics listed below.

Patience ---Bravery ---Exercise ---Discipline

To become the LEADER you need to be - that you know you *can* be - you need to have **patience** with yourself because improvements in your day-to-day business will not come about overnight - they will come more quickly than you might think, but not overnight. You will need to practice consistent patience with your team, because individuals respond at different rates. They can all improve, but the rates of improvement will not be equal.

In order to obtain your meeting goals, you are going to need to implement changes, and for the most part these changes will occur within yourself. In order to change your personal status quo - the way you are used to thinking - you will need huge reserves of **bravery**. It is human nature to resist change, right? Or is that really true? Perhaps not - in fact, no! Want proof? Look at Charles Darwin's theory of evolution. If it were human nature to resist change wouldn't we all still be living in caves and ignoring the advent of that round thing we call a wheel? The nature of human beings is not so much resistance of change as it is resistance - or fear - of the unknown. This fear is healthy; it is what has kept man surviving and progressing through the ages, but you need to make this fear work for you! So you need a steady dose of bravery which will allow you to try new things, to step out of your current comfort zone and boldly go where you have previously feared going. It's called the PATH TO SUCCESS. Trust me, you can do it.

At this point we are thinking we can be patient and we can be brave. Now we need to implement **exercise** in order to put this new positive thinking into action. Here we are exercising not our biceps, but our minds. We need to flex the gray matter and exercise the parts of our personalities that are weak. Remember we need you to become the mentor and motivator who LEADS the field. This means you must locate those weak areas within you, and strengthen them by trying them out, over and over again until it becomes second nature for you to publicly compliment a worker who has done a good job for instance, or who has voiced a smart idea. No magic or faking will do here either - you must be genuine in your delivery or your efforts will be worthless.

The last of the requirements is **discipline**. Pretty obvious really - in order to make this program work for you, you will require the discipline to not only read, but to actually study this book. You will need discipline to absorb and practice what you learn, in progressive steps, and the discipline to keep trying, even when your staff do not respond at the pace you would like them to. All things come to he who waits. That doesn't mean wait and do nothing though, it means nothing pays like persistence. Try, try, try to discipline yourself to avoid reverting back to your old ways, even after you see results of this program but find yourself in a moment of weakness or frustration. DO NOT let yourself slip back into the mindset of the regular meeting! We will give you techniques specifically designed for these moments, erasing your temptation to blame a poorly prepared meeting on a lack of time ever again!

So before you go further into this manual, are you satisfied within yourself that you possess the confidence to believe you can read, learn and change, thereby becoming more successful? Would it help if you realized that no one human being was born a super manager or a super meeting presenter or a super leader? In the same way, no one human being was born an Olympic swimmer, or a champion bodybuilder. These things are learned with hard work and practice, building your confidence over time. Does this mean there is no short cut, no easy way? Yes, unfortunately it does. Nothing worth having comes easily - if it did it would hold no value for us!

How do you eat an elephant? One bite at a time! So knuckle down and study this manual, and you can become a better leader.

CONFLICTS

When conflicts arise between staff members, it is best that they be resolved *outside* of the meeting. Such conflicts must, however, be dealt with ultimately and it is important that you do not shy away from handling these situations. Let's spend some time on this now, because whenever diverse individuals are thrown together in a work environment there will likely be personality clashes, and this is something that you will definitely need to address at some point. Left unresolved such issues can have serious consequences, but you can turn them into a win-win situation by dealing with them in a timely fashion.

Let's say there are two staff members who have a conflict and there is resentment building. Left alone, what is likely to happen? Each of the dissenters will have their own following of "allies", some of whom want to become embroiled in the goings on, and some of whom will prefer to be left out of it altogether. Either way, a large-scale eruption is inevitable. As the manager, your meetings will become an arena for opposing sides, and opinions will be aired which can distract and divert the planned course of your meeting. This is why we need to address this common situation and learn how to tackle such opportunities when they arise.

Once you become aware of the problem, discuss it in private with one of the parties, letting them know at the outset that you are aware of a problem involving them and that you want to see a resolution - quickly. Take charge: if they insist this is a personal issue and not something to be discussed with you, advise them that what may have started as a personal problem has evolved into a work problem, as it is affecting the jobs of those around them, and this is why you, as the manager, need to intervene. Advise them you will be speaking with each party separately, followed by a closed-door session involving both parties and yourself. Chat with each person, listening and remaining neutral, then get the two together and BE IN CHARGE. Advise them at the outset that the reason for discussing their behavior is centered around their work performance, as well as that of those around them. Stress that you will not tolerate unnecessarily harsh interactions, nor the spin-off factor this creates for their team members. Inform them that the reason you are taking the time to help resolve this situation is because you value them both and want them to remain members of your staff. Further inform them that a positive change needs to occur for the good of the department and that if they can't implement such a change themselves then you, as manager, will make changes by whatever means are necessary. At this point you should have their attention.

It helps if the root cause of the grief can be established, and most times there is one party who feels aggrieved by the actions of the other. For instance, Person A did or said something, possibly innocently, which was misconstrued by Person B, who was offended, and a grudge was formed. Escalation of such a situation is easy from this point, since the two work closely together and have lots of opportunity to display anger, letting day-to-day business provide them with a forum for acting out.

More often than not, when you approach a situation like this in the manner described above, both parties are happy and relieved that the air has been cleared, and are visibly lifted. At this point they are very likely happy to shake hands and move on.

Another common type of conflict occurs not in the form of blatant acrimony, but in a more subversive manner, wherein one party comes to you to complain, privately, about another. This could be a similar case to the one previously described, but at an earlier stage. This is a perfect opportunity for you to take action early.

Acknowledge the concern, and make a written note for your records (do this while the "complainant" is still in your office). Once they have fully aired their concern, give them the following challenge. If you have noticed any unusual behavior from this individual, let them know now. Then give them the prescription to resolve the pain, borrowing, as we do here, from Dale Carnegie. Tell them now that they have identified their concern, you expect them to utilize their personal and interpersonal skills in a sincere attempt to turn this situation around. The thought of doing this will likely horrify them, but this is all the more reason for you to issue the challenge, providing you with an arena in which to coach and follow through with them.

Begin by suggesting they ask the other person to talk about what they perceive as a problem. Possible suggestions: "I know we didn't hit it off very well ..." or "I know we disagree over the ..... issue, but I would like to get things back to a professional level because I value the experience you bring to this team and I think we will work more efficiently if we can pull together ...". This may be perceived as eating "humble pie", but putting yourself in this person's place, we're sure you will agree that it's not easy to act disrespectfully in the face of a professional approach like this one. It is highly likely - in fact we have seen it happen - that a situation like this will be resolved with a professional, lasting trust and appreciation between the two previously opposed parties.

Dale Carnegie said:

"Any fool can condemn, criticize and complain and most of them do! ... Instead of condemning people, let's try to understand them. Let's try to figure out why they do what they do. That's a lot more profitable and intriguing than criticism; and it breeds sympathy, tolerance and kindness. To know all is to forgive all"

PART II
LESSONBOOK

1
KNOW THE COMPETITION AND KNOW YOURSELF

In the timeless business and leadership novel, "The Art Of War", Sun Tzu suggests, "… know the competition and know yourself and you will never lose in battle".

All the great leaders of our day know this to be true. Andrew Roberts, author of "Hitler and Churchill: Secrets of Leadership," describes very accurately the differing styles of the two leaders when he writes, "Churchill knew very well what Hitler was like, but Hitler had no idea what sort of man Churchill was". Of course, we all know the tragic conclusion of that complex relationship.

If you know yourself but not your enemy you might win half the battles. If you know the enemy but not yourself you might win the same half again. But it is only in having both sides of the information that you will be fully armed to win every time.

This adage has been used many times in business since its words were first written around 2,500 years ago in ancient China.

A professional speaker and author once said: *The successful man is one who finds out what is wrong with his own business before his competitors do*. This is certainly one way to ensure a competitive edge. How does one find this out unless they do some competitive shopping?

A potential problem with today's employees is that they can get tunnel vision through knowing the strengths and weaknesses of their own business, but not those of their competitors. Why would they go anywhere else for their automotive needs? Why would they go anywhere else for their electronics needs, vehicle needs, clothing needs, dry-cleaning needs, or any needs that are equivalent with those provided at their own place of work? Well, because they want to know their competition!

Competitive shopping can be an eye-opening and rewarding experience for today's savvy employee.

One of the most successful training courses I offer is called the Technician Customer Service Excellence course. During this course I try to teach the automotive technicians (mechanics) what it is like to be a consumer who is dropping off his/her vehicle for repairs. I frequently ask the attendees: "When was the last time any of you took your vehicle to a business other than yours for service?" You can probably guess how they answered!

"Are you kidding – why would we do that when we can service our own vehicles?" I might take this question one step further and ask the same group of technicians: "When was the last time you had someone come over and fix something in your house?" More often than not I am given a similar response: "Never!"

These guys are the last of a dying breed of "Mr. Fixits". They don't have to hire service people because they can do it themselves. And yet, these are the same employees who are oblivious to the anxiety people feel when they bring their vehicles to the dealership for repairs, because they never put themselves in that exact same position.

Competitive shopping is worth doing with your employees, if only because it will help them to understand what the customer experiences within their own establishment. The other great benefit is that if employees are sent shopping, having been "armed" by their manager with specific questions and duties, they can report back with information that will be of definite use within the dealership, in potentially countless areas.

Every employee should partake in competitive shopping. Many sales meetings falter because of repetition, which can only lead to boredom. That's why involving as many staff members as possible in every facet of the meeting makes for a very enjoyable and rewarding meeting. Therefore, if you choose to employ a strategy like competitive shopping, try to make sure that everybody gets a chance to participate. This will guarantee not only increased interest in the next meeting, but more contribution also.

Many retail managers and owners pay keen attention to competing stores. I know of many store managers and owners who, when on vacation, will drop in to businesses within their marketplace to see what's going on. They might check out everything from signage to interaction with staff – how were they greeted? What products were on display?

Why do retailers do this? It's because they are passionate about their business. Robert Kiyosaki, in his book "Rich Dad, Poor Dad", describes true passion as both love and anger combined. I remember speaking with a young woman once. She was in college – 19 or 20 years old. I enjoyed conversing with her because she spoke deeply and passionately about her career choice to be a child counselor and social worker. She described vividly her own youth, which had, sadly, been overshadowed by physical and sexual abuse. She chose this career because she had passion for her past. She was angry - because of the suffering she endured as a youth. But she also developed love that she wanted to project onto other boys and girls who found themselves in a situation with which she was familiar. I know this girl is going to provide invaluable assistance to the many lives she will touch during her career.

The experiences of your employees may not be as dramatic as those of this particular person, but any negative experience tends to stick with us, even those which are small or insignificant in the grand scheme of things. Therefore, a worker who has been on the receiving end of truly incompetent or insensitive service, and has been left feeling upset by it, will be much more likely to make a sincere effort not to inflict such an experience on his or her own customers.

In order to enhance the experience of our customers, we must continually strive to increase the quality of the service we provide. This is the whole idea behind the Japanese drive for success and betterment, known as Kaizen. The principle of Kaizen is to continuously improve business practices by eliminating waste.

Let's look at the pros and cons involved with sending our employees out to practice "competitive soul searching".

Pros

1. The employee is given the ability to learn first hand what the competitor is doing, rather than hearing about it second hand from the manager during a meeting.
2. It can break up the monotony of routine business and give the employee some renewed zeal in his/her job.
3. The employee can be given a forum during a future meeting to discuss what he/she has learned from practicing competitive shopping.
4. The employee feels good about going out and spending someone else's money. Oh, by the way - did we mention that you may be required to hand over your credit card or a little cash in order to ensure that this exercise is as effective as possible?

Cons

1. Your employees may not know exactly what to look for when they embark on their competitive shopping mission. This is why, as their manager, it is your duty to provide them with details for their assignment. Have an outcome in mind relating to how business can improve as a result of your competitive shopping exercise.
2. They can find out that the competitor is a better place to work, and quit!
3. The employees, on their return, may be fully capable of sharing their experiences with you, in the comfort of your office, but may feel uncomfortable illustrating their ideas in front of a group. Understandable, considering the anxiety most of us suffer in the face of public speaking. Solution: See to it that the first couple of employees chosen to execute this task are people who are comfortable speaking in a group. (One thing I learned being a Toastmaster™ is that people flub up on public speaking because they do not typically know enough about the subject matter at hand. This should not be the case here. The employee should have all the information they

need about your company – all that is required of them is to discuss the similarities and differences they noticed between your company and the competition.)

4. You're out of pocket some money - Cheer up! It should be tax deductible.

 Toolbook ref. Chapter 1

2

EMPLOYEE INVOLVEMENT IN MEETINGS

Every employee should play a part in Sales Meetings throughout the course of the year. Many Sales Meetings falter because they offer the same information, provided by the same facilitator, falling on the same deaf ears. That's why getting the staff involved as much as possible makes for a very interactive and dynamic meeting.

A. Competitive Shopping

The lucky employee who was recently appointed to do a competitive shop should be briefed by the Manager prior to presenting his/her case at the Sales Meeting. If we are going to ask the employee to speak up in front of a group, it is essential we "tee them up" prior. This will enable them to effectively present what they observed in their transaction(s).

Observe: To see, notice, and note the difference.

Here is how a typical conversation should transpire between the Manager and the employee prior to the meeting:

Manager: John, I'm going to ask you a few questions about what you experienced when you were competitive shopping. What was your overall impression of _____?

Manager: What day was it/What time of day was it?
(This will reflect whether it was a busy day or a slow day – the same level of service should apply no matter what day it happened to be.)

<u>Manager</u>: Recount each stage of your visit beginning with the greeting and ending with your conclusion of business.

<u>Manager</u>: In the meeting, I am going to ask the staff to share their feelings about your observations, in particular what you felt were the competition's strong points and weak points. Try to come up with a list of the top 5 strengths and the top 5 weaknesses you observed.

B. Mystery Shopping

Mystery Shopping can be done a number of ways. One of the best ways is to "arm" an outside person (preferably with some knowledge of the industry) so that they can effectively partake in your mystery shop. Your briefing should include providing them with a list of the top 5 items that your company sells. With this information in hand, the shopper can go out and commence shopping at your place of business, as well as those of your competitors. Mystery Shopping is usually videoed, voice recorded or both.

Once the Mystery Shopper has compiled the relevant information, you can review the results with your employees. Do this without identifying the unlucky victims - the staff will often know who you're discussing anyway!

Next, engage your staff in conversation about what they felt were benefits of the exercise, and ask them to suggest ways in which their own performance, or that of a specific department, could improve as a result. Utilizing Mystery Shopping in any business can provide a much-needed wake-up call for both management and staff by providing us with a fresh look at how we are perceived by our buying public.

C. Facilitating the Meeting

Facilitator: One who is skilled in providing an environment for others to learn, to easily persuade, to allow or to make easier and more convenient any training offered.

A Manager should be a Facilitator and not a Manager during employee-involved Sales Meetings. Remember, the main focus of the Sales Meeting is either to inform or to motivate - that's all!

We must also remember that the Sales Meeting is not a forum to expose or pick on any one person - this should always be done in private, never in a group. The Sales Meeting is not to be mis-used as a "bitch session". If we can't come up with solutions, then we shouldn't be bitching anyway!

Let's say your department finds itself embroiled in a major heat score and your staff has just been read the riot act. What happens next? Heads are held low, the tone is somber, and employees are sulking. They feel the severity of the situation. Now let's move on! The Facilitator must be able to turn this mood around. Think of ways to do this which involve your staff – ask one of them to recount a situation wherein a heat score was turned into a customer service triumph. Let them remind themselves of what an effective group they can be when they really try.

We have all been in meetings which consisted of barely more than the Facilitator preaching endlessly. The feeling this approach generates amongst staff can be similar to that of a child who is being lectured by a parent. And the resultant sentiment is too often on par with this picture: The words of the authority figure become nothing but white noise in our heads, and they are completely tuned out! If we're going to spend the time to conduct a meeting in the first place, why not make an extra effort to ensure that it is effective and rewarding for everybody?

Let's ask the employees questions throughout the meeting. This keeps them on their toes as well as making them feel valuable to the team, the overriding message being, "Your opinion is important to the successful operation of this business".

 Toolbook ref. Chapter 2

3
KAIZEN

The Japanese have a business term which is synonymous with *continuous improvement and elimination of waste*. In order to enhance the experience of our customers, we must continually strive to increase the quality of the service we provide. This is the whole idea behind the Japanese drive for success and betterment, known as Kaizen. The principle of Kaizen is to continuously improve business practices and eliminating waste. Leave it to the Japanese to possess a term which is equivalent in meaning to "non-complacency".

Any company in any part of the world would benefit from cultivating this sort of mentality within its workforce.

Many North American companies don't give as much credit to their employees as they should, even though these same employees often know the ins and outs of their jobs and the company they work for as well as, or better than, their superiors. They may, in fact, be in the best position to determine ways of making improvements to the business, but might hesitate to voice these ideas for fear of being thought of as someone who "rocks the boat". They also may worry about reprisal from superiors who, unfortunately, often feel threatened by an "underling" who exhibits a desire to improve business. This kind of negative thinking can only have a detrimental effect on the company as a whole, and should never be tolerated. Whenever forward thinking is demonstrated in the workplace, it should always be praised and never feared.

Along with the problem of managers feeling threatened by an employee who rises to the top or introduces ways to improve business, is another potential roadblock to growth through employee input. Revisiting something we discussed previously in this book, under the heading "Leadership", we know there will always exist managers, in all types of businesses, who resist implementing changes because they fear change itself. These managers have immense trouble separating themselves from the mindset, "But it has always been done this way". The ability to be open-minded is crucial if you want to successfully introduce a Kaizen strategy to your staff.

Kaizen is not something that should be taken lightly, for it has the potential to save a company thousands if not millions of dollars per year. It is well worth looking at ways in which to implement Kaizen in *your* workplace.

Kaizen in the workplace can result in:

- Savings of time
- Savings of manpower
- Savings of staff turnover
- Savings of energy
- Savings of resources
- Savings of space/real estate
- Savings of unnecessary waste

Promoting a Kaizen mentality in the workplace pays many additional benefits to employees as well as employers. Take, for example, an assembly-line worker installing widgets on a stereo component. If this employee knows there is a better way to perform this task which has the potential to save the company time, money, and resources, yet the employee is fearful of bringing it up, eventually he will become frustrated in his job. He may feel his manager doesn't give him enough credit for the job he does, or he might feel that, in general, this is a poorly run organization, which doesn't deserve an employee like him. Either way, he is extremely likely to eventually quit this company, or get himself fired.

Is this the fault of the organization or the management?

As difficult as it is for many managers to hear this, it is nonetheless true: *People don't leave organizations - they leave managers.*

So, Kaizen can also:

- Improve employee turnover rate
- Improve morale
- Create a healthier, more fun working environment
- Decrease staff sick days
- Increase overall efficiency

How do we foster this kind of Kaizen thinking amongst our employees and managers? Easily - it all boils down to WIIFM: What's In It For Me?

Some Japanese companies have gone so far as to employ a policy similar to this one: "Any Kaizen change which is implemented as a result of an employee suggestion, saving the company a tangible amount of energy, resources, and/or materials, will result in the employee's receiving half the amount of the company's overall savings for either 6 months or 1 year." I have heard of some very significant Kaizen programs which resulted in hundreds of thousands of dollars in company savings, and a nice bonus to a forward-thinking employee!

 Toolbook ref. Chapter 3

4
MAKE IT EASY

We should always be thinking of ways to reduce our customer's stress by making it easy for him or her to buy our product. Ensure that it is pleasant to deal with your people and your company. But how can we do this? There are many ways, and a good starting place is to be the expert that people think of when they need advice. This strategy is exactly the reason that many companies offer their employees discounted prices on merchandise and services. When staff members own and use the products they are selling, they are easily able to speak knowledgeably and convincingly about the qualities and characteristics of these items.

Removing stress also means making it easy for the customer to buy. How annoying is it for a consumer to be required to give redundant, repetitive information time after time? Customer Service is all about making it easy on the customer, and yet some companies - banks and airlines for instance - tend to request and require certain information before they will even allow you to pose your question! You call their Customer Service department, enter a 16-digit account number, and then a pin number, and still you haven't even spoken with a live body! Then when you do get to speak with someone, they ask you for the exact same information you have already given! This is frustrating - today more than ever when the average consumer has an extremely busy life and limited time.

The photo-finishing industry has gone through a large upheaval lately. Everyone from Eastman Kodak down to the local photomat has been affected. Why? Two reasons: Mega-retailers entering into the business, thereby decimating the "Ma & Pa" photo-finishing industry (Why make a separate trip to an independent shop when you can have your film developed as you shop for groceries and clothes for your kids?), and the mainstream use of digital cameras.

Consumers today, more and more, are purchasing digital cameras, enabling them to take and download pictures on their home computers, all without the use of film. These pictures can even be printed at home, using a color printer!

In order to combat these challenges, one nation-wide chain of photo-finishing shops set up a computer program designed to track customer habits and purchasing patterns. For instance, if Mr. Jones normally requests 5x7 format with cropped edges, as well as duplicate copies, the employee, checking the customer's shopping history in the computer, can ask Mr. Jones, "Did you want it your usual way - 5x7 size, cropped with an extra print?" Yes!

This pays dual benefits: It tells your customers that you care and that you are familiar with their shopping needs. It also saves customers time and the inconvenience of repeating a familiar request.

Keep in mind: People are creatures of habit, and this is no less true where buying habits are concerned.

How do we make it less stressful for our customers to conduct business with us?

Make it easy for them to contact your business: 24-hour phone numbers; toll-free numbers; direct lines; email address and web site, etc. Make it easy for them to buy: consider adding a web store; make sure you accept all popular forms of payment; offer deferred payments.

Make it easy and comfortable for them to walk into your store and browse without harassment.

It takes a significant upheaval to change someone's loyal purchasing patterns. It usually requires a very bad customer service experience or a substandard-quality product, resulting in a negative situation which wasn't properly remedied by the seller.

 Toolbook ref. Chapter 4

5

QUESTIONING THE CUSTOMER

Ask probing, open-ended questions. This will help to ensure that your customer provides all the information you need to successfully match your particular product to their needs and wants. This puts you in a better position to recognize and specify which features of your product should be emphasized. Accomplishing this task requires good listening skills as well as the knowledge to properly structure your open-ended questions.

Examples

- *How* often do you plan on using ...
- You said you had a similar model before and you want to upgrade now - *what* features did you like/dislike on the one you had?
- *Who* other than yourself might be using this ...

Use the 'how' 'when' 'what' 'why' words to begin your questions.

Open-ended questions cannot be answered 'yes' or 'no'. These questions begin with 'who', 'what', 'why', 'where', and 'when'.

Some of the questions listed here will feel natural to you and you can practice using them in your work. **Circle three or four** *that you feel most comfortable with and make them part of every reference interview you conduct.*

1. What kind of information on _____ are you looking for?
2. What is it you want to know about _____ ?
3. What would you like to know about this topic?

4. What do you mean by _____ ?
5. Would you tell me more about ... ?
6. What else can you tell me that might help us locate materials?
7. Could you tell me what you're working on?
8. I'd be interested in knowing ...
9. Would you explain ... ?
10. Is there something specific about _____ that you are look-ing for?
11. Would you explain that to me in more detail?
12. I'm not certain I understand ... Can you give me an example?
13. I'm not familiar with _____ .
14. What examples can you give me?
15. What do you already know about _____ ?
16. Do you know some key concepts, terms or vocabulary for this topic?
17. Where have you checked for information so far?
18. What would you like to know about_____ ?
19. When you say _____ , what do you mean?
20. Can you describe the kind of information you would like to find?
21. If I could find the perfect book to help you, what would that book have in it? Or, what would the title be?
22. Where did you hear or read about _____ ?
23. How will you use the information? That will help us with our search.
24. I'd like to help you find the best possible information. Can you tell me more about your subject?

(Thanks to Carol Leita for "The Reference Interview: Asking All the Right Questions, Spring, 2002". This material has been created by Carole Leita and provided through the Infopeople Project [http://infopeople.org/], supported by the U.S. Institute of Museum and Library Services under the provisions of the Library Services and Technology Act, administered in California by the State Librarian. Any use of this material should credit the author and funding source.)

One manager I know has made it a policy in his Service Department to ask new customers whether they would mind filling out a quick questionnaire. I know what some of you may be thinking: "Isn't that imposing on the customer?" Kind of like those annoying telemarketers who insist on calling your house during dinner?

Not so. In fact most people are very obliging to the employee who makes the request, and after all, it is done face to face. Most customers find it much more difficult to say no when the person asking is right in front of them, especially when that person puts forth a polite and professional manner.

Of course if the employee makes this request in such a way that the customer feels put upon, then it's not going to work. The request must be worded carefully, its message impressing upon the customer the employee's desire to gather information that will help them save time and money down the road.

The question could be worded like this: "In order to serve you better and more quickly in future, would you mind if I ask you a few questions about how you prefer this service?"

Think about it - who doesn't like to be asked about their personal preferences, especially if their providing this information could save them time, money and inconvenience on future visits? As in previous chapters wherein we discussed different approaches to Customer Service, this is yet another way for your employees to go about "making it easy for them to buy".

Features and Benefits

A successful, proven technique in Sales is to demonstrate the features and benefits of your product to your customer.

Feature

Explain individual details of your product that on their own may or may not be unique to that item, but in any event are items worthy of note. Demonstrate what each feature does, how it works and why it is there.

Benefit

Describe to your customer what each feature can do for them, eg, save time or save money, or provide more value or durability in the long run. Explain how this feature has the advantage over that of your competition.

Work this technique into your sales consultations in order to build a value and quality story about your product.

 Toolbook ref. Chapter 5

6

CUSTOMER'S PERCEPTION IS REALITY

What the customer sees and perceives is what he or she believes. It's as simple as that.

Perceive: To become aware of, through the senses.

This means the customer's perception might be different from one person to another, however, things that influence the decision-making process often have little or nothing to do with the facts about a product or service. The sales environment, the business environment and the salesperson's appearance and demeanor will all greatly contribute to the customer's 'perception' before any facts about your product are presented. The purchase decision is being formed before you have had the chance to open your mouth.

Motivational speaker Tom Peters describes how part of a customer satisfaction survey conducted by one of the world's top airlines yielded an amazing 'perception' when it came to the aircraft engine maintenance. The survey result showed that coffee stains on the fold-down tables meant to the passengers that the engines were not well maintained. How could this be? The passenger's senses formulated a concern with their immediate environment. This vague idea developed into an opinion and, when asked about the overall maintenance of the aircraft engines, many customers responded negatively, even though they had absolutely no factual data with which to support their feelings.

The perception boiled down to this: If the flight attendants could not or did not keep the cabin tidy, then surely the mechanics and support crew couldn't be performing their jobs that well either.

This illustration works at every level of the selling and buying cycle. Prospective purchasers - often subconsciously - will use all their senses to form opinions that have a strong influence in the buying decision. This means you have to help create the right environment in order to yield the best results.

Employee Appearance

Employee dress code can certainly be variable depending on the product or service offered. The general rule of thumb - although it seems unnecessary to have to point it out - is to always wear clothing which is clean and in good condition. After that, what you wear should reflect the business you are in, the products or services you sell, and the marketplace you are operating within.

- A salesperson working in a clothing store should represent the products from that store.
- A furniture store's employees might best don professional business attire.
- A stereo retailer would dress according to the demographic breakdown of its clientele.

In any event, you can always be overdressed and still fit in well. If you are underdressed you will stand out much more than you will fit in. You can always become more casual by leaving your suit jacket undone, or loosening your tie but you can't do much about upgrading your level of dress once you have left home.

It's important to note that the use of company uniforms has been increasing in popularity over the past couple of years and, according to information on this subject, these are not our parents' uniforms! Many companies previously thought of as "too upscale" for uniforms, including banks and corporations, have introduced the concept as a way to increase brand advertising and give the perception of unification. The adoption of uniforms also helps your company to present a professional appearance, as well as eliminating the chance of a rogue staff member dressing in an embarrassing manner!

Appearance of the Display Area/Showroom

Carl Sewell, one of the most successful Cadillac dealers in General Motors' history, wrote a book entitled, "Customers for Life". In it he devoted a whole chapter to describing how important clean restrooms are to his business. He sums it all up by saying: ***"Why would you ever want to give someone a reason - even a subconscious reason - to question doing business with you?"***

Many automotive dealerships utilize floor-to-ceiling mirrors in their showrooms. Why do they do this? Is it to give the perception that the dealership is bigger - a trick of the trade commonly employed by interior decorators? Perhaps. But the truth is that when a customer is sitting in a vehicle in a dealership showroom and they can see an image of themselves in the vehicle they are considering for purchase, then subconsciously they have taken a mental step toward ownership.

Appearance of Product or Service.

When you spend $300.00 on having your car repaired and you look under the hood only to find the engine is just as dirty as when you drove into the garage, how does it make you feel? The perception is one that prompts the customer to ask this question: "Did the mechanics actually do anything to my car? Because it looks the same." Many dealerships offer a complimentary car wash to help eliminate this false notion.

 Toolbook ref. Chapter 6

7

BUILDING RELATIONSHIPS

Many people find it very easy to build clients as friends. Some people are blessed with the ability to quickly and easily connect with other people.

When you are genuinely interested in another person, it's hard not to become friends. In the timeless classic, "How to Win Friends and Influence People", Dale Carnegie said that in order to win someone as a friend, you should "be hearty in your approbation and lavish in your praise". In other words, be aware of the person you are dealing with; acknowledge and commend them on their tastes. How do you accomplish this without sounding insincere? The number one most important rule is to pay attention to the other person. Consider what they are saying, what they are wearing, the style of their speech, the automobile they are driving, and information they share about their children, their interests, hobbies, and habits. All of this helps, because people, no matter what their age, religion, sex, or creed, love to talk about their own interests.

Of course, we have all run into people whose sentences all seem to begin with "I", "Me", or "We". Be cognizant of how boring it is to be on the receiving end of conversations like these, and how pompous and self-absorbed such people sound.

A general truth in building relationships is that common denominators must always be established between the parties involved.

How do we find out about common denominators? Through:

- *Communication skills*
- *Confidence*
- *Open-ended questions*

Forge that Relationship

Strengthening and building relationships is certainly one of the best ways to improve overall customer retention. "Superstar Salespeople" try to establish relationships and rapports with people they are trying to build as long-term clients.

This can be done in a number of ways. If time permits, talk to a customer about things other than business or personal needs.

Sometimes a subject for other interests can be triggered by what the person is wearing, what they're driving, or through conversation with their peers. To a lesser degree it sometimes helps to know their approximate age in gleaning clues to their likes, dislikes, habits, hobbies, and interests.

As a Sales Manager, how do you teach your staff lessons on building friendships and rapports with customers?

Define the difference between demographics and psychographics so that the staff is fully aware of what these terms mean and how they relate to your business.

Demographics

The statistical analysis of populations, showing sizes, occupations, sex's, martial status, incomes, education levels etc.

Psychographics

Graphic representation of the personality traits of individuals which include their hobbies, habits, lifestyle activities, recreational activities and so on.

A common trap which many salespeople fall into is thinking that they know the customer well enough so that after the sale has been made they can still remember subtle nuances about that person days, weeks or months after the sale has taken place.

Rule #1: You can never know your customer well enough! Inexperienced as well as veteran salespeople forget that "people buy from people they like". Even seasoned sales veterans can be browbeaten into thinking that price is always the chief issue in a sales transaction, when for many customers, the relationship between themselves and the salesperson, as well as the trust they place in that person are much more important factors in making a sale.

If your company negotiates in business to business transactions, it is even more critical that you know your client and their psychographic information. Good managers should reinforce with their staff that it's not always about who's got the best price, or better selection, or the more attractive pricing terms. It's about the people, and the service these people are committed to provide, now and in the future.

Exceptional service like this is a result of taking the time and making the effort to know and remember the important aspects of your customer. Remembering that John likes to sail his 40-footer on Lake Erie, or Richard likes to shoot a couple rounds of golf each week, or that Mary's son Joey is trying out for a National Hockey League team next month are all things that matter to the client. Remembering these seemingly minor details is what separates a good salesperson from a superstar salesperson.

 Toolbook ref. Chapter 7

8
PRESENTING MERCHANDISE

How a product is presented in a storefront or on a shelf will have a direct relationship to how well that product sells. The same can be said about how a salesperson holds a piece of merchandise to be shown to a customer. The manner in which a salesperson holds and presents an item gives a direct and indirect message as to how valuable that product is. Picture an antique store and how delicately its merchandise is picked up and passed to a customer for inspection and appraisal. The same kind of respect and care are demonstrated at high-end clothing stores - the kind of retailers who sell names like Armani, Versace and Valentino. These businesses spend untold thousands on packaging and presentation of their goods in store and window displays. Consequently, when a salesperson presents these garments to a customer, they are handled as though they were sewn with golden thread.

(Conversely, when an industrial piece of equipment is displayed its value is more easily appreciated if it provides potential customers with physical access, allowing them to touch and handle it.)

Many retail businesses spend vast amounts of money on packaging and presentation of their goods in store and window displays. Nordstrom's American retail chain is an impressive example of how displaying and merchandising helps sell items.

A typical problem encountered by salespeople in a retail setting is that they lose their objectivity for displayed merchandise when they see it day after day and week after week. High-end clothing retailers know the value of displaying their merchandise in the most flattering light, but they also know that "changing up" this merchandise on a regular basis keeps it, as well as the entire retail area, from looking old or stagnant. This practice is especially important in appealing to clientele who tend to visit your business frequently.

Has your business designated someone to be responsible for changing up the merchandise displays? Does it need to?

Do your fixtures and displays motivate salespeople to present merchandise enthusiastically, urging customers to buy?

If not, you may consider arranging a visit by a professional merchandiser to objectively critique your merchandising displays and offer recommendations for improvement. In some cases, it is not necessary to go to these lengths. Who knows? You may have the perfect person for this task right in front of you. Check with your staff to find out if anyone in particular is interested in aesthetics - perhaps an amateur interior decorator, or someone who has studied merchandising in business school. You might be surprised at what you can accomplish by tapping into the unknown talents of someone already on your payroll!

The other big question to ask when considering merchandising impact is: Does the primary displayed item urge the customer to buy it, as well as secondary items?

A professional salesperson should always be thinking of items which will complement the principal item being marketed for sale. Just as a clothing retailer provides accessories for a business suit (ties, shirts, pocket squares, belts), so should a parts person selling a valve-cover gasket provide complementary items like silicone and gasket strippers.

The salesperson should never just verbally ask the customer if they would like to consider complementary items; instead these items should be retrieved by the salesperson and displayed next to the principal item under consideration, in this case a valve-cover gasket.

If you are selling clothes, for example, and your customer is buying a new suit, you should mention that your shop has a sale on combination dress shirts and ties. This gives the customer a chance to realize some savings in purchasing something they will appreciate using with the original purchase, and at the same time you will increase your $'s sale per customer.

Note: Always offer the best advice to your customers. Maybe today your best advice is that the customer does not in fact need an extra item they were inquiring about. Your candid honesty and professional attitude will be rewarded through repeat business over a long term. Compare this to what you may have risked in pushing an unnecessary sale on someone for a quick dollar (and some guaranteed business for your competition in future). Today's customer will appreciate (and may even be surprised by) your help, and not only will they very likely return to you for future purchases, they will also refer new customers to you.

A professional salesperson always has "down time". Use these occasions to create lists of complementary items which can be displayed as add-ons to the principal items you are marketing.

When the customer says, "Yes, I'll buy them", what should the salesperson do next? Two things: Number one, shut up! (That is, of course, unless he or she can offer the customer some useful advice regarding operation/servicing of the product, or purchase of complementary items not yet discussed.) The second thing is, write up the order and don't try to justify the sale. This can become a route to unwinding the deal you worked so hard for, and can lead to the customer changing their mind. So be quiet and take the order!

 See Toolbook ref. Chapter 8

9

MEET AND GREET

You only get one chance to make a first impression.

The greeting sets the stage on which the whole transaction will take place. The first encounter with the customer should always be that of a greeting rather than, "Can I help you?" This tells the customer that you are at their service, willing to help, but it also provides them with some assurance that you will not "get in their space" unless invited to do so.

Greeting

Although rudimentary, these are some foolproof examples. (before you criticize them, compare them to what is currently happening in your store!).

- *Welcome to _____.*
- *Thanks for coming in, my name is_____. Is there a particular area I can direct you to?*
- *Please call on me if you have any questions.*

Disney Corporation has a Greeting policy for *all* their staff to adhere to, most would agree that their customer service reputation is stuff of legend.

Let's take the time to acknowledge everyone who walks through our doors. Prestige Ford, in Garland, Texas, has achieved the status of #1 Ford Truck dealer in the world and #2 volume Ford dealer in the world by incorporating and practicing what is known as the "ten foot rule". This rule enforces that any staff member who comes within ten feet of a guest in their dealership acknowledges, greets, and says hello to that guest.

Many businesses aren't using the word "customer" these days; they substitute the word "guest". For example: Petro Canada's service station staff refer to their patrons as guests, and wear name badges that identify them as "guest services" personnel. After all, isn't that the feeling we would like to impart to our valued customers - that of being a guest in our home, and of expecting to be treated as such?

Southland Corp. - the parent company of 7-11 - instructs all their employees to greet and acknowledge every person who comes through the doors. Wal Mart® has a similar policy of meeting and greeting. As a matter of fact, Wal Mart first introduced the "Greeter" as an in-store theft deterrent. Now the person who holds this position at Wal Mart acts as a customer service representative, information provider, and problem solver.

You don't have to be a mega-store or large chain store to implement a greeting policy for your employees. One company I worked for had one or two female greeters on from morning until night. Their job was to welcome the customers as they walked into the showroom and introduce them to a salesperson. Part of the greeter's job was to qualify the customer as best she could, enabling her to introduce the customer to a salesperson whose specific skills or characteristics most closely matched the needs of that person. Obviously this extra effort increased the store's potential to close that customer.

Your greeting should be cheerful, polite and brief. There is nothing worse at any stage of the sales process than insincere or forced statements. Make your customers feel sincerely welcomed, and *always* practice your lovely smile with that greeting. Whenever possible, use the customer's name.

"The sweetest sound to the human ear is that of their own name."

- Dale Carnegie.

 Toolbook ref. Chapter 9

10

ENTERTAIN THEM

If you can keep people laughing and having fun, then inevitably they are going to enjoy doing business with you. Penner Men's Wear store in Lethbridge, Alberta is a great example of having fun in the workplace.

What kind of customer interaction might you witness at Penner Men's Wear?

A lady comes in looking for a suit: "Come on over here, Mrs. Henderson - let me show you what we have for your husband in the Tent and Awning collection." Mrs. Henderson, of course, giggles about the size of her husband. And voilà, the mood is set!

Of course, not everyone would be able to get away with this kind of comment. A familiar, jocular relationship like this results from repeated dealings with a customer whose personality and sense of humor are well known to you, because of the time you have invested in them.

Donald Cooper (from the Cooper Sports Equipment family) knew this very well. He set up a women's clothing store warehouse in the growing, northeast part of Toronto. He knew of the boredom factor that men often experience when on a shopping trip with their significant other. He installed reclining seats and large-screen televisions in close proximity to the store's waiting/changing area. This enabled the women freedom to shop to their heart's content without feeling pressure from the presence of an impatient husband! The happy outcome of this strategy was that the men were kept entertained and, sure enough, sales increased. Keep customers in your store longer by entertaining them and they will spend more.

The best salespeople make their customers laugh using impromptu humor. Keep your customers laughing and having fun, and guess what? They will return to buy merchandise. Old Man Penner was aware that when a customer is shopping, he or she is really just seeking an expensive form of anti-depressant. So, knowing that people want to be brightened up, he made it easy for them when they entered his store. Mr. Penner knew that if people were having fun they were much more likely to loosen their purse strings.

Fun Workplace

Workplace - dull or fun? Fun at work and a high-performance team are not mutually exclusive. They are very often the hallmark of a well-run, efficient business. To put your customer first, you must really put your employees first. It's been said before, but a happy employee reflects all good qualities of a company and its products. Conversely, a customer can sense poor morale through the employees' actions and attitudes. Inevitably, lower profitability will be the net result.

An example of a highly successful corporation where fun is mandated: WestJet Corporate Head Office in Calgary, Alberta. The signs in the office are a bit of a giveaway! The Accounting Department sign reads, 'Beanland'; the Executive area sign reads, 'Big Shots'; and the sign marking the Human Resources Department reads, 'People Department'.

WestJet's 'Big Cheese', Clive Beddoe, says, "We have fun. If you're not having fun, you're fired. People are most productive when they enjoy going to work. If they can have innocent fun, why wouldn't you do that to make it more enjoyable for them?"

Workplace humor can relieve stress, increase productivity and help keep valuable employees. Staff turnover is expensive and counter-productive. Keeping turnover to a bare minimum is well worth the effort.

Obviously putting your customers first is a goal, but to accomplish this, *you must put your employees first.* Sound like a contradiction? Not at all. You have to understand that if each of your staff members is to treat customers as their #1 priority, they each have to be happy in their work, and they must feel job satisfaction. They need to know that their manager respects them, backs them up and holds them in high regard. They must always be acknowledged for their contributions to the team effort. (Remember, love me or hate me but don't ignore me).

At Stadium Nissan in Calgary, Dealer Principal Lawrence Bates will go out and buy ice creams on a hot day then hand them out to his Technicians. On a cold day he will get them hot sausage rolls. Dealer Principal, Glen Richardson, of Charlesglen Toyota in Calgary, has been known to show up on an employee's moving day with his truck and cube trailer to help lend a hand and actually load sofas and boxes. What do you think these actions do for promoting satisfaction with their staff?

ESI (Employee Satisfaction Index) has been recognized and promoted more and more frequently in the last decade as a fundamental requirement in business operations. Large corporations put huge resources into measuring and improving their ESI and for good reason: *their people are their biggest asset.*

 Toolbook ref. Chapter 10

12

MENTAL PREPARATION PREVENTS POOR PERFORMANCE

Flashback: Oct 30th 1974 Zaire - "The Rumble in the Jungle"

Picture, if you will, Muhammad Ali shadow-boxing on the day prior to the big event. The fight of the decade - no, of the *century* - is about to take place less than 24 hours from now. The fighter is locked in mental concentration. He is bobbing and weaving, throwing uppercuts and jabs as if his opponent is right in front of him.

George Foreman, his rival, is actually miles away, in a different compound, yet to Muhammad Ali he exists before him. What was Ali doing? Why? He was mentally rehearsing his upcoming duel for the World Championship boxing crown. Ali was visualizing every facet of his game; every obstacle that had potential to get in his way, and every move his competitor might utilize to impede his success.

In what was to become England's most significant sporting triumph since 1966, the England Rugby squad was well on their way to Rugby World Cup victory in November 2003 during the England vs. France semi-final game. The commentator was heard to be saying, *"...as he visualizes the fate of this ball..."*, just as Jonny Wilkinson eyed the goal posts for what seemed an eternity but was only several seconds. He could see the flight of the ball in his mind's eye and, from a difficult angle, successfully converted the goal kick. England won that game and went on to win the final, thanks to the accuracy of Wilkinson's ball-kicking. Every time he set up to take a penalty kick, you could see the mental preparation Wilkinson was going through, to the point where the commentator recognized and talked about it. This visualization produced nothing less than world-class success.

Any serious athlete knows that mental preparation prior to an event improves his/her ultimate performance. Visualization of maximum performance can be key to realizing your greatest potential. Is this practice limited to athletes? No. Many professional salespeople do it as well. Whether driving to their next appointment, preparing to dial their next client or simply waiting for their next retail customer, the professional salesperson should be mentally preparing for their next opponent like Muhammad Ali or George Foreman.

The professional salesperson should mentally map out the sales process from "greeting" to "goodbye". If he or she fails to do this, then sure as God made "buyer's remorse", inevitably, important aspects of the selling process will be missed.

I can recall many situations wherein I concluded a meeting with a customer and immediately thought to myself, "Shoot! I should have said this", or "I should have done that". Losing opportunities "in the moment" can be eliminated through the consistent practice of mental mapping. We should visualize possible objections and how we will overcome them. We should visualize presenting the merchandise, demonstrating the features and benefits and how this relates to the customer's needs. Mentally rehearse the entire sales process, with no shortcuts, right through to asking for the order.

 Toolbook ref. Chapter 12

13

ADD CREDIBILITY TO WHAT YOU SAY

They say there are two major factors that prevent people from purchasing a product or service. No need and/or no money.

Let's look at this. Sure, if there has been no need established by the consumer, then of course it is highly unlikely that he or she is going to pull out a credit card and make a purchase, especially a large purchase.

So let's assume there is a need - and money is the same important issue that it always is.

My theory is that people buy for *these* two basic reasons: Trust and Information.

First, let's assume you have a customer who seems mistrustful - of you, your staff, your business or the information you have provided. How does this happen? In almost all instances it can be traced back to something we have said, or neglected to say, in the customer's presence. Keep in mind that at any given time, your mouth can be your best friend or your worst enemy.

I know that I am leery of anyone who promises the moon and stars for whatever product he/she is selling. Their product, their company, their warranty is, of course, "the best", and the competition doesn't even merit consideration. Don't get me wrong - as a good salesperson you should always promote your products or services as the best choice for the customer. But, the information you provide must *always* be kept within the boundaries of reality if your goal is to inspire confidence and trust.

The best salespeople are those who establish trust and credibility by talking very favorably about their products but also by providing the customer with honest, candid feedback about the product - ways in which it will meet their needs, but also ways in which it may not. Sometimes the issues which detract from the product are minor and won't inhibit the sale; otherwise though, the customer will be pleasantly surprised by your candor and honesty and will remember this positively in future.

In this way, you will be building long-term credibility and trust with your customers.

The second major factor to consider in a customer's buying or not buying is information. They either don't trust that they have been given enough information with which to make an informed decision, or they feel they have been given the wrong information. Always ensure that you are providing the facts correctly when counseling your customers on your product - and if you aren't sure, tell them you want to double-check, and go get the facts! Remember, when you are providing information to a customer, they are calculating how much they can trust you, as well as your word.

Adding credibility to what you say does not come from adding more words. It comes from showing customers third-party testimonials and using tools that speak about your company and its products, like:

- Printed information providing third-party accolades
- Published trade or consumer articles
- Information from other sources web sites
- Reference letters from other companies

Do you have credibility tools that are available to your sales staff? If not, why not?

 Toolbook ref. Chapter 13

14

STAY AHEAD OF THE CUSTOMER

Staying ahead of the customer has everything to do with integrity, and doing what you say you are going to do.

If you say you're going to arrive at 3 o'clock, get there at 10 to 3. If you say you're going have that proposal by Monday, make sure it's there on Monday. If you say that it's going be fixed by 2 o'clock and ready to go, don't wait till 2 o'clock to call and tell them, "it's not going be ready until 2:30".

Case in point:

I was given a specialty camera from my father, a Hasselblad®. It is a mechanical format camera that takes unique film. Only a select few dealers sell and process the film. I was unfamiliar with this fact until I went to a couple of photography stores and neither one had the film, nor the equipment required to process it.

So, I had to drive across town to a select Hassleblad store, where I discovered that indeed this specialty retailer sells the Swedish cameras; however, they do not develop the film in-house. The film would have to be sent out, by them, to a lab that is equipped to deal with Hasselblads and their needs. The sales clerk assured me that my film would be ready for pick-up in five days. I neglected to ask the clerk if he meant five calendar days or five business days; however, I gave him the benefit of the doubt and arrived on the sixth business day. Lo and behold, after driving across town to pick up my developed film, I discovered that it was not ready!

The sales clerk with whom I dealt on this visit placed blame on the film processing equipment, the couriers, the other employees - in short, she assigned responsibility to everyone who could possibly have been involved in this unfortunate transaction except, of course, herself. I recognized this as a classic case of "buck-passing", which impressed me not in the least. After all, my arrangement was with her and with the business she was representing - no one else's involvement interested me, or mattered to me. I remember thinking to myself, "Lady, don't start pointing fingers! Accept the blame, apologize for the inconvenience I have undergone, and then move on".

So I left unhappy, and photo-less, but with a pledge from the clerk that my photos would most assuredly be ready the following day. So I returned the following day - and again, no luck!

By this time I had been inconvenienced not just once, but twice! And to make matters worse I had received no apologies and no phone calls from this business; just broken commitments, finger-pointing and buck-passing.

In the end I spoke with the store's manager - who did apologize to me - but by that point I was, understandably, beyond satisfaction.

If we screw up in our jobs, then it is up to us to "'fess up" and make every possible effort to replace the customer's lost time. If we make promises we can't keep, it is imperative that we determine a way to lessen the customer's inconvenience - quickly! Richmond Honda, the largest volume Honda dealership in Canada, operates under the following policy: If they screw up and don't get a customer's car fixed on time - as promised - they will pick up the customer's car from their house or office and then drop it off to the customer after repairs are properly completed. This is customer service! They are trying to compensate for some of the customer's lost time.

Referring back to my photo-finishing catastrophe - the store manager did end up dropping off the pictures to my house when they were complete. It was the very least they could do!

The lesson here is, "If you screw up – 'fess up"!

Furthermore, any change to the original expectations of the customer, as set by you, requires further follow up. This boils down to respect and integrity. If the product is due to be delivered on Tuesday, and we learned the previous Friday that it had been delayed in shipping, creating a 2-day variance from the original arrival date

- don't wait until Tuesday to contact your customer. Let them know *as soon as you know* about any changes which will affect their situation.

Under-promise and over-deliver makes the customer happy!

Under-promise and over-deliver could mean:

- Price quoted is more than price charged
- Delivery time is sooner than expected
- Model upgrade beyond what they ordered
- More product or service provided and not charged for
- Courtesy follow-up after the sale

 Toolbook ref. Chapter 14

15

TAKE CONTROL

The more time you spend with an individual customer, the better your chance of making a sale. Time alone is not the only factor crucial to the sales process. This is why it is essential that a Manager educate his/her staff on the benefits of being fully in control with each and every customer. In the absence of a controlled environment, it is much too easy for your customer to come in, shop around, assess and compare prices, and then bolt!

The more time you spend with your customer, and the more involvement you have with them, the better your opportunity to build *obligation*. The more obligation, the better the likelihood of making a sale. This is certainly the case for large ticket purchases like automobiles, homes, recreational vehicles, and boats.

This principle is the same whether selling products or service. For instance, a computer company whose salesperson invests a significant amount of time in a customer during the purchase process is likely to realize a long-term service contract for computer software support. This is due to the obligation factor mentioned above - the more time a customer spends with a salesperson the more obligated the customer feels to reciprocate. In this way, the customer makes a psychological commitment to the person who has provided them with what they consider to be quality service.

Building obligation is so important that Automotive Profit Builders®, a training company for automotive dealerships, promotes building obligation by giving the prospective customer a small gift just for shopping at a particular dealership. Usually this is in the form of a small token like a key chain, tire gauge, or a minor parts department accessory. This gesture of giving imparts a psychological obligation to the prospective customer even before they have sat down and negotiated the purchase of an automobile.

The principle of taking control is important in business, but keep in mind that it is a somewhat delicate operation. If the customer feels forced to spend more time than they want to with the salesperson, they may feel pressured to enter into a sales transaction that they are not ready for, to the point of feeling uncomfortable or imposed upon. Taking control does not mean handcuffing yourself to the customer. It is a more subtle process, which involves controlling the conversation - asking the right questions, directing the customer to look at different products, sharing pertinent information with the customer and, in cases where the customer is not yet ready to purchase, ensuring you obtain their name and phone number so that you can keep them apprised of any information that will assist them in their search.

Another important factor to consider when using the "Take Control" theory is that it is bound to be much more effective when used with customers who are shopping in your business - on your turf, so to speak - than during a sales visit by you to their place of business. In this case it is to your benefit to relinquish a measure of control, as you may be perceived as pushy.

 Toolbook ref. Chapter 15

16
RULE OF THREE

All too often, salespeople who are in the process of trying to secure a sale, manage instead to talk themselves right out of one. As the old saying goes, "We have two ears and one mouth for a reason!" We should listen twice as much as we speak. Listening to your customer is just as important in the exchange of information as what you tell them. Remember that people are capable of absorbing only so much information at one time. The Rule of Three can help you to orchestrate your conversations in a way that allows you to get across the important points you need to make without over-informing the customer to the point where they tune out or become bored.

One of the greatest and most valuable tools taught at Toastmaster tm is the Rule of Three.

The Rule of Three consists of breaking communication down into three parts:

1. Opening
2. Body
3. Conclusion

The Opening

The principle behind the Opening is much the same as what we learned in primary school English. Its purpose is to grab the attention of the listener with the first line or initial statements.

Sometimes this is referred to as a "hook" statement - although in formal training circles it is an "I.B.S." or Initial Benefit Statement. Whatever you call it - it is designed to capture the listener's attention so that they will continue to be interested in what you are saying.

In sales scenarios this might:

1. Address a problem or a need
2. Save the client money, time or resources
3. Speak directly to the interests of your audience

The Body

This refers to the "meat" of the subject matter. It generally brings together a few different ideas in order to achieve a desired result.

During the Body portion of our presentation, we should be prepared to offer three reasons why a particular product or service will benefit the customer. Any more than three is overkill (too much information), any less than three is not credible enough. THREE IS JUST RIGHT!

The Conclusion

The Conclusion is a call to action. At this point we are offering information as to why this is the program or product that is right for you, as well as providing you with the steps by which to acquire it.

The Rule of Three turns up in other areas as well. Consider the options we find offered in all sorts of retail establishments. The most commonly used are:

1. Small
2. Medium
3. Large

Another set, more frequently used in the sale of tires:

1. Good
2. Better
3. Best

How about payment options:

1. Cash
2. Check
3. Credit card

The sales process:

1. Features
2. Advantages
3. Benefits

A successful example of the Rule of Three stems from a period of time I spent selling Sales Training Programs. The courses were illustrated on a promotional page that summarized the training I was offering. I repackaged my training programs into 3 volumes and offered 3 benefits for each volume. My closing ratio increased from around 25% to 75% through my presenting programs this way. Every dealership across the country needs help to improve sales, customer satisfaction or employer/employee morale.

In order to make shopping as simple and straightforward as possible, all companies should offer their most important and most commonly purchased items/services in groups of three. Added on to these simple, itemized lists should then be further choices related to these items.

Compare automotive marketing strategies. Let's look at Toyota, Honda and Nissan. These manufacturers typically offer three different trim levels per vehicle with three different option packages for each model.

There are numerous benefits to this strategy of simplification. Manufacturing costs come down, because the factory is only running three styles versus literally hundreds. Inventory costs come down, allowing quality control to improve.

Also, simplifying your product/service "menu" means an automatic decrease in the chances of your salespeople slipping into "information overload" when dealing with customers. This way, the salesperson can instead spend time talking to the customer about the top three benefits and how they relate to the customer's needs.

Give your customer "Three Reasons to Buy Today".

 Toolbook ref. Chapter 16

17

MAKE A NOTE

As discussed in Chapter 7, Building Relationships, it is common for salespeople to believe they will retain valuable information about a customer for days, weeks or months following a sale.

As soon as possible, immediately following each transaction or discussion with a customer, a salesperson should record the pertinent details of the conversation, including notes about the customer and the topics discussed. These notes should be kept in such a way that they can quickly be accessed. Tools useful to this practice include personal devices like a Palm Pilot, or a CRM program (customer retention management) in your computer system. Make special note of the "hot-button" items for each existing and potential customer. Include any personal data you obtained during your interactions with them, such as hobbies, habits, family situation, etc. (see Chapter 17).

Time Management Systems That Work

Individual as well as team success depend on a combination of many ingredients coming together at the right time and in the correct ratio. Being organized on a personal level is one of those main ingredients that you cannot do without. There are many types of time management systems available to you and your team, and each person needs to decide on one that will work for them. You can use your PC, handheld electronic organizer, paper diary - whatever suits you best. Just discipline yourself to stick with it. If you use your system with success your team members will want to emulate you by following your lead. Just remember, if you decide on using an electronic system - make regular back-ups!

Be efficient with your paperwork. Teach your staff how to be efficient. Too many managers leave their staff to flounder in this area. Tackle it early with them and get them working with good habits.

Handle paper as quickly as possible. If you pick it up, do something with it - read it, file it - done. Read it, circulate it - done. Read it, reply to it - done. Maintain neat files, both in the file cabinets and within the folders on your desk. If you want to lead by example, the appearance of your desk must have a positive impact on your staff when they come into your office. It's unrealistic to expect them to be very organized and time-efficient when you appear not to be.

The widely acclaimed business book "Seven Habits of Highly Effective People" by Stephen Covey, discusses the benefits of writing down weekly goals versus the traditionally taught daily goals. Mr. Covey imparts that people should outline their goals divided into: Personal and Business. Create balance in your life, set goals and make sure you write those achievements/goals down so that you see them frequently and start living them.

Recommended: Palm Pilot, PDA Systems, Microsoft Outlook

"The weakest ink is better than the strongest memory."
- Mike Rolland

 Toolbook ref. Chapter 17

18

UNIQUENESS

One of the cardinal sins in the selling of a product or service is to disparage your competition in order to make your own business more attractive in the eyes of your customer.

Unless you have sole ownership and/or rights to a product or service, you have competition. Vehicles, houses, stereos, clothes - you name the marketplace and the customer has options. So how do we best handle this competitive environment? Rather than spend time and energy trying to detract from your competition, highlight the unique characteristics of your own business, its services and products, and convey to your customers why it is in their best interests to purchase from you.

Your sales team should be made fully aware of all the benefits available to their customers, and the ways in which the particular products or services you offer distinguish your business from others. If your staff are well armed with this information, they can comfortably pass it on to their customers without ever feeling the need to slight other businesses in their industry.

It's all well and good for you, as the Sales Manager, to spout off, illustrating at length all the reasons that your store and its services are great. But isn't it better, and more rewarding, to have your salespeople share *their* opinions in this area?

For instance, have every salesperson come up with their own reasons describing why this location is the best. Why do you offer better sales service? Why are you the best sales team? How do you offer enhanced customer care? You can collect everyone's answers and create a master list for the staff to read and discuss. This list could be written out on an overhead or a whiteboard, or be made into a PowerPoint presentation. In this way you will likely find that together, the staff will come up with more positive reasons to promote their business than you could have accomplished on your own.

Undoubtedly some of the staff members will be "bumps on a log" - unable or unwilling to add any relevant information as to what makes this location and store better than the competition's. In a case like this, it is the manager's job to present some sub-topics that will encourage and promote discussion amongst *all* staff members.

What separates one sales outlet from another? Assuming *ceteris paribus* - same market size, same products, equal number of staff - why would one location consistently outsell the other?

Answer = THE RIGHT PEOPLE

How do you get the right people?

Hire for attitude, then train and coach for experience.

You, as a manager, must make a consistent effort to stay abreast of developments within your industry. Attend training sessions and read relevant material. Keep yourself open to constant learning, and pass this knowledge on to your staff, in tandem with the rote tasks of their daily work. If you keep these items in mind, you will be well on your way to hiring the right people.

Coaching

Manager, mentor or friend? You don't have to seek approval or friendship in your position of leadership. If you lead by example, if you work hard, others will follow. Put your feet on the desk though, and you will tear down any trust and belief that your employees had in you. (Why should they work hard when their leader doesn't care and doesn't appear to do any work himself?)

We recommend regular short sessions with your staff wherein you can each talk freely, one-on-one. Encounters like these are essential in nurturing a strong relationship and improving morale.

Mistakes

Each of us is used to being spoken to by a supervisor anytime a reprimand is in order. If one of your staff members makes a decision that turns out to be wrong - in other words, a mistake – the last person who needs to be informed about it is the person who made that mistake. As their manager you will need to talk to them about the error, but make it brief. Read "The One Minute Manager", by Kenneth Blanchard. He promotes a one-minute scolding, not the ten-minute lecture that most of us have experienced. Talk about the mistake – *briefly*, and then move on to discuss ways in which we all can learn from the experience. Go on from here to talk about the positive attributes this person brings to your team.

Touch Me

No, most definitely not literally, but talk to your salespeople frequently in a coaching capacity. It is far worse to do nothing and say nothing to your staff over a long period of time than it is to frequently admonish them. People would rather have some contact and interaction with their supervisor - even bad interaction, than none at all. So here is your opportunity to build the best team by utilizing frequent coaching exercises.

MMFI: Make Me Feel Important

Dr. Glen Pfau, President of Communication and Management Professionals, uses this acronym to explain a basic human need. We all like to hear praise, but we also need to hear something about our specific performance, as each of us is an individual who needs to be recognized as such.

Coaching and Training

So what is the difference between training and coaching? When do you coach, and when do you train?

Use the following to guide you on the correct path:

Step 1: Observe salesperson's activity and performance.

Step 2: Do they have the appropriate skills to accomplish their goals?
   - If you answered yes, then coaching *may be* required.
   - If you answered no, then training *is definitely* required.

Step 3: Do they have the necessary skills but still are not performing to expectation?
   - If you answered yes, then coaching is required.

Step 4: After either training or coaching has been implemented, go back to Step 1 above. The cycle is continuous.

Coaching

Coaching consists of brief talks with an individual, and the potential benefits are limitless! For example:

- Improved morale
- Improved attitude
- Higher confidence levels leading to improved performance
- Growth in overall job satisfaction leading to higher productivity
- Manager's investment of short but regular sessions, sometimes lasting mere minutes, for a valuable payoff in the long run

Training

Training is demonstrating a skill and teaching an individual to become proficient in that skill. This means allowing them time to learn, to practice and to develop the skill. If needed, outside consultation could be provided.

A rookie mistake will cost you at least one game every year.
                                        - NFL Analyst

A rookie mistake could cost you at least one customer every day.
                                        - Dave Skrobot

 Toolbook ref. Chapter 18

19

FOLLOW UP

Follow-up is an absolutely crucial aspect to the success of anyone who wants to make a career of selling. It is those salespeople who keep the best contact with their clients and prospective clients who will win most often. There are two different ways to break down follow-up. Firstly, there is the type of follow-up that is carried out where a prospective client has exhibited interest in your product, but has not yet purchased. The second form of follow-up occurs after the sale is completed.

Depending on the sales process, pre-sales follow-up can occur for weeks, months and even years prior to an actual purchase taking place. Usually the size of the purchase has a direct relation to how much pre-sales follow-up is needed. It is those salespeople who persist and persevere who will win in the end. Isn't this true about most aspects of life?

Persistence: Try, try again.

Perseverance: Persistence with grace.

Patience and perseverance are so important that in the Harvard Business Review, Oct 2003 issue, the Eight Key Principles of doing business with the Chinese are described, with patience and perseverance listed as elements *key* to success.

An old business saying states:

"Tell them, tell them again, then tell them what you told them."

A very crucial step in pre-sales follow-up should occur immediately following our meeting with a prospective client, in the form of a follow-up letter, including a proposal. The follow-up letter should express three key elements.

The first element thanks them for spending the time to meet with you, and giving you an opportunity to compete for their business. The second part reiterates their needs and describes the means by which your company can satisfy those needs. The third part lays out, in detail, the steps by which the preceding proposition can be accomplished. In other words, how are we going to satisfy the customer's needs, and within what time frame?

Perhaps Step #3 will look something like this:

1. We can offer Item A at a reduced price for 3 more weeks.
2. We will telephone you one week from today.
3. We hope to consult more with you on the 21st of this month.

Note: Your follow-up letter can contain a special offer which is available for a limited time. Don't be afraid to create urgency! Give yourself an opportunity - and a reason - to contact your potential customer again.

Let's face it. It is human nature to put things off and to avoid making decisions quickly. Therefore, if we can help to persuade the potential customer to act quickly through thorough and timely follow-up on our part, then our chances of making a sale are greatly improved.

Consider offering:

1. Attractive terms
2. Discounts
3. Added Value: "Purchase now and also receive ..."
4. A preferred price on installation and/or service
5. Increased trade-in value

Point Number 5, above, is popular in the retail automotive

industry. Have you ever heard something like this when shopping for a car? "Mr. Customer, I just overheard another salesperson say that his customer is looking for a used car like the one you are driving. If you're still in the market to buy a new car, we might be able to step up and offer you more money for your trade." Talk about creating urgency!

AFTER-SALES FOLLOW UP

Any significant purchase of a product or service should be followed up with a courtesy call.

When should this be done? The timing can depend largely on the type of product or service in question. The point is - *make the call!*

As a general rule, within one week of the sale or the delivery of the item is an appropriate timeframe. However, maybe your own company policies reflect monthly or quarterly follow-up, or:

- On the anniversary of the purchase
- On the customer's birthday
- On a special event in the customer's interest
- New model launch with better/more features

 Toolbook ref. Chapter 19

20

HOW TO HANDLE OBJECTIONS

What is an Objection?

An objection is a statement the customer makes to notify you that he/she requires more information in order to make the decision to purchase.

Many experienced salespeople love to hear objections. For them it is a challenging opportunity to provide further information to an interested customer, and no less a chance to close the deal. Objections are feedback, of a sort, which tells them the customer is still interested in discussing options and ultimately wants to make a purchase.

For this type of salesperson, an objection is the customer's way of seeking more information, and is accepted not as a roadblock but as an opportunity.

I love to hear objections, and had my share of them as a sales trainer. A typical objection would be: "We, as representatives of 'Anytown Motors', must present staff training according to corporate criteria, so why would we spend money on yours?"

"Great!" I would think to myself, recognizing an opportunity to enlighten my potential customer as to the reasons my program was different or superior.

My favorite objection was, "I think it's too expensive". Perfect! This would allow me to assume an accountant's "close" wherein I would proceed to grab a pad and pencil and calculate the potential savings or profit to the customer, should he decide to hire my services.

Objections, as we have previously established, are the customer's way of seeking more information. They are giving you an opportunity to persuade them that making this purchase is the smart thing to do, and that once they have all the proper information, they can feel confident in finalizing their decision.

I like to ask the following question to people in a group:

"What are the three main reasons that people won't buy?"
Invariably, I hear many different responses:

- They don't have the money, or they're on a budget - something financial
- They don't have a need for the product or service
- The salesperson hasn't assessed the customer's needs properly

The truth is that none of these statements is wrong; however, I believe it boils down to two simple truths. 1) The customer does not have enough/correct information, or 2) they lack trust in the person or persons providing the information.

Common Objections

Common objections might come to you in the form of, "I want to think about it …" or, "I'm not sure - let me check with my partner before I decide …" - or any of a multitude of other statements you may be familiar with!

Remember, these statements are either objections or they are *excuses*.

Excuses are just that. They are not "real" objections, but merely a stall for time or an indication that the customer cannot buy without losing face.

If a person cannot afford to make the proposed purchase, for instance, they may use an excuse as a means of protecting their pride or ego. A salesperson, as he/she gains experience, will become more and more proficient at separating an excuse from a valid objection.

Remember that, when faced with an objection, there is a right way and a wrong way to handle it. The right way is based on the *Rule of Three* (see Chapter 16).

Cushion, Rephrase, Solve

1. Cushion the objection
   Use an empathetic statement like, "Yeah, I know how you feel".

2. Rephrase the objection
   Repeat back to the customer what he/she is expressing, "Yes, $500 is a lot of money".

3. Provide a solution.

"You can buy tires for less than $500 but for the type of driving you do, and considering the length of time you plan to keep the car, higher-quality tires will provide you with the best performance and cost you less in the long run."

The way a customer's objections are handled can make or break the closing of a sale. When one is brought up, an objection must be acknowledged and dealt with. Do not ignore objections - learn to treat them as an opportunity to demonstrate the features of your product. Use the objection as a starting point, listen well to the customer, and then present him or her with a question that restates the question they have posed. You need to discover the underlying concern for the objection. Use probing questions to get the customer talking. This will put you in a better position to respond to the challenge and turn what began as a negative into a positive.

You can build from there using the 'features and benefits' technique. When you have covered the objection to the customer's satisfaction, don't be afraid to ask if there are any other concerns. This will confirm to the customer your confidence in the quality and value of your product and it will put you in a stronger position to approach closing the sale.

 Toolbook ref. Chapter 20

21

THE SELECTION PROCESS

One of the biggest challenges that exists in selling is knowing how to "narrow down" a variety of options in order to present your customer with the ones which best suit his or her needs. By using the sales tools learned in this book, you can improve your qualification skills, enabling you to spend your time and energy on the right product or service for each customer. This method is known as the selection process.

The selection process is all about asking the right qualifying questions of the customer. This is the one time that the salesperson *should* ask an abundance of questions without feeling this may lead to the customer's feeling overpowered. In fact, the customer will appreciate knowing that the salesperson is genuinely interested in ensuring his needs are met. So use all the "who's", "what's", "why's" and "how's" you need to in order to get the information that will allow you provide the best fit possible.

Of course, there are possible pitfalls to the selection process. The two most common are:

1. Providing insufficient information or choices, so that the customer's interest is not suitably piqued.
2. Providing too much information, resulting in the customer's feeling confused or overwhelmed.

The first problem may not be the salesperson's fault if it is happening on a regular basis. It is the responsibility of the management team to ensure that the inventory carried is competitive within the marketplace, providing the sales staff with a reasonable selection of merchandise or services to offer their customers.

The second potential problem is a more likely occurrence and it is often a result of over-exuberance on the part of the salesperson. This type of over-the-top excitement can easily lead to what's known as the "More is More" (MIM) complex. The "More is More" complex occurs when the salesperson presents too much information about the product or service at hand, and/or offers too many choices. The customer inevitably becomes overwhelmed and begins looking for a reason to leave, taking with him your opportunity for a sale.

It is the narrowing-down of the selection which in many cases is the most difficult task to successfully accomplish in sales. So here we need to apply the psychology of selling, as well as the psychology of words, in order to provide ourselves the very best opportunity to help the customer make an informed decision.

Take for example these two scenarios:

"Most of our customers feel that this _____ product is the best value."

Versus:

"A customer told me recently that he feels that this _____ _____ product is the best value."

The difference is obviously subtle, but which one has more impact? Many people think they want to be leaders and pioneers, but the simple fact is when it comes to purchasing pricey items, people don't want to feel alone. If they made what later felt like a bad purchase they may be prone to feel regret. On the other hand, if they made what they feel was a good purchase - and a popular one - then that's okay and they won't be as likely to suffer buyer's remorse.

Salespeople have told me that they may not want to use a statement like this one if it isn't in fact 100% true. Understood! There are other word choices you can make if you are in a situation different from the one demonstrated above:

- A friend of mine …
- I myself own/want to buy this product …
- Many people with the same needs as yours opt for this …

But keep in mind, nobody wants to be the one buying the Pet Rock® if no one else has gone before him or her!

 Toolbook ref. Chapter 21

22

TELEPHONE FUNDAMENTALS

A very common concern that many Managers deal with has to do with how telephone prospects are handled. The management or owners of a business usually find out first hand how bad it can be when they themselves call the business and are treated haphazardly on the phone. They may be left on hold for an eternity, treated discourteously or be met with a departmental runaround. It happens all too commonly in business today, and most of us have been on the receiving end of it. Imagine that this is the reception your sales prospects are subject to when they call your place of business, hoping to enact a transaction.

Many companies have policies in place that address ways in which to answer the telephone professionally. However, after a period of time, lethargy can set in amongst the staff, and professionalism is all but forgotten. One firm that I worked for had an excellent script that the staff adhered to religiously in the beginning. Within four months though, the wheels fell off the bus in a big way, and what started out as, "Hello, Denny Andrews Ford, Sales Department, Frank speaking", became, "D.A. Ford, Frank here", or even worse, "Sales Department".

The greeting is often not the only problem. Consider these glaring mistakes:

1. Neglecting to ask for the order
2. Neglecting to set up a firm appointment
3. Neglecting to control the conversation (forgetting to record the person's name, phone number, and other pertinent data)
4. Not building rapport by seeming uninterested or unfriendly
5. Not elaborating on the unique strengths of the company, instead focusing on price and price alone

6. Neglecting to thank the customer for their call and their patronage

Let's look at these in more detail:

1. Neglecting to ask for the order

    Many times the caller will have the salesperson running around, fetching prices and availability, and double-checking inventory, after which he or she is not even invited to come in, or to hold the product with a credit card.

2. Neglecting to set up an appointment

    The value of the order and the availability of the product should reflect the urgency with which an appointment is made. Eg., table lamp vs. leather couch. Generally speaking, larger-ticket items should necessitate obtaining and confirming an appointment.
    And it is so easy to do. It can sound like this: "...I am in on Fridays, Saturdays and Sundays - are any of those days good for you to come in? Great! Morning or afternoon? Great! We will see you at 3 o'clock on Sunday, Mr. Smith. Let me get your phone number to confirm and to call if there are any problems on my end." This illustrates the most important aspect of telephone skill, that of taking control.

3. Neglecting to control the conversation

    You must earn the right take control. If you have checked stock, checked pricing, and checked availability, doesn't it make sense that you have earned the right to get something from the customer? Let's make sure that we get some pertinent data, if nothing else, so that we are able to inform the customer, for instance, that the item(s) they were inquiring about have just been sold, thus saving them a trip.

4. Not building rapport

    Generally speaking, the more time you have spent with a customer over the phone, the more obligated they will feel to come in and purchase from you. If time permits, keep the customer talking and ask them questions relevant to the product or service they are inquiring about.

5. Elaborate on the strengths of the company rather than price and price alone
    Make sure to point out the other aspects of what makes our company great. This could be years in business, warranty and return policies, the owner's reputation in the community, free installation, loyalty purchasing program, whatever applies. (See Uniqueness, Chapter 18.)

6. Not thanking the customer

    We should always end the call with, "Thank you for choosing _____", or, "We appreciate your patronage...." This sets the tone for future relations and is a just a polite way of ending a call.

 Toolbook ref. Chapter 22

23

COFFEE CLUB

Joe Girard, the World's Best Salesman (Guinness Book of World Records), coined the term, "Coffee Club" to describe a common activity for workplace "slackers". The coffee club consists of salespeople who sit around, sip coffee, and gab with other coffee clubbers about sports, the weather, and myriad other time-wasting topics. These are the same folks who complain consistently that business is soft and money is tight. According to the popular saying, "Some people make things happen, some people watch things happen, and some people say, What happened?", the coffee clubbers are the people who watch things happen. Conversely, there are those staff members who refrain from joining the coffee club. Instead, they stay in their offices during slow times, making follow-up calls and cold calls to leads they have acquired by working hard and making the most of their time. These salespeople might find ways to obtain names of people who are selling their cars; they might visit the service department to carry out some research on customers with older cars and large repair bills. These people exemplify another old saying: "Successful people are those who make a habit of doing things that other people don't do."

Joe Girard's point, in placing emphasis on habitual timewasters was, quite simply, don't fall into the destructive routines that entice unmotivated salespeople. Instead, keep yourself *motivated* by making full use of every working minute to expand your area of sales opportunities. While the average salesperson indulges in idle frivolity, get your brain engaged in making things happen - and make *this* your daily habit.

The difference between *fairly* successful salespeople and *very* successful salespeople in terms of sales production is not necessarily a huge amount of volume. Imagine taking your average and above-average salespeople to the next level. If they could each increase their sales output by 20% on a regular basis, they would be much happier with their increased commissions and you, in turn, would be a whole lot happier with the total gains. We can't make more hours in a day but we can make optimum use of every day, and disbanding the coffee club is one sure way to discourage a slack attitude when customers are not knocking your doors down to buy your products.

What helps to create a winning attitude amongst ours sales staff? Part of it is teaching our team how to be different than our competitors. For example, when I was a fledgling office-furniture salesperson, there were a number of companies in my area competing hard for their own slice of the pie. This local competition included two of the country's largest manufacturers complete with highly-trained, professional sales teams. As an outside salesperson I was to visit the office towers downtown on a daily basis, armed with catalogues and price sheets describing our vast array of office furniture. Normally these small- and medium-sized firms employed a specific person whose responsibility it was to purchase the company's supplies and equipment. Like so many salespeople in so many industries I felt like I had been tossed into the deep end to flail and make cold calls with minimal training in this area. As you can imagine, this led to instant frustration.

The first weeks were especially trying since I expected people to drop everything as I arrived unannounced, and spend time with me to discuss their office furniture needs. Think again! It didn't happen that way at all and I found that these people had either an existing need, or - as in most cases - none at all. Keeping that in mind, I decided to "make it easy for the customer to buy" and provide them some added value they were not expecting.

So, every day I would assemble two identical files, legal and letter- sized hanging files labeled "OFFICE FURNITURE (NEW AND USED)". Now when I was cold calling I would ask the receptionist or office manager if they had any present needs. If they said "no", I would still go on to tell them that we offered 200,000 square feet of office furniture, new and used, including free delivery on minimum orders. I would leave with them a catalogue with my business card attached, already enclosed in a hanging file ready to be filed for future use. Think about this for a moment - what happens to the majority of catalogues, price lists and business cards you receive from salespeople making cold calls? One of two things: they either go straight into the recycling bin or they are thrown to one side for a few days or weeks, and then discarded.

What happened to my hanging files? Having provided the file size I knew they used, I would ask them to keep it in their file cabinet for future reference. When I then made my follow-up phone calls, I would ask them if they still had my file for reference and thank them for having met with me. I would ask (as if I didn't know) what color the hanging file was that I had given them; with the excuse that I wanted to make sure they had the latest price list. This would mean they would likely open their drawer to look at the file (I could often hear them lean across to their file drawer and check!). I used unusually-colored folders that would stand out in the maze of stored files. This little reminder with the follow-up call was often enough to secure sales for me in the future. What was different about what I had done compared to what other salespeople had done? I made it easy for them to file away the information without creating clutter in their office. I helped them organize what might otherwise have been junk mail. I stood out in their minds as having done something different and having considered their needs so as to make it easy for them to search for the type of product I was selling when they eventually made a decision to purchase. And the mere fact that I had given them a bright blue file to sit amongst their existing mass of manila files made my product stand out even more. A simple thing, but done with regularity and follow- up, this strategy provided me with an ever-increasing customer base who came to request me by name.

The company I worked for received these requests for months and years because of the success of my outside-the-box sales tactics. My name was on their minds when they needed service. I had not joined my office "coffee club"; instead I had spent my time creating distinct yet simple sales aids that paid huge dividends over the long term.

This is the same principle we should teach our salespeople. Think outside the box and discern new ways in which to make it easy for our customer to buy, reducing some stress in their lives (see Chapter 3). A great salesperson will do things that the competition or other salespeople on the team won't do. Let's not let our new salespeople fall into the rut of the other coffee clubbers.

The mere fact that you are already reading this book is a significant sign that you are not a Manager who is content with being average and ordinary - you want your sales team to be Superstars. So, foster in them that willingness to be unique and special, and to want to separate themselves from the coffee club!

Here are some other ways we can teach our salespeople to avoid the lure of the coffee club:

- Re-visit and re-connect with past clients
- Re-contact unsold prospects
- Follow up on leads found on the company web site
- Visit the local library and search out new leads
  - Eg,   New home listings
    New business licenses
    Business-to-business and Retail
    Directories, like www.infousa.net and
    www.infocanada.ca

 Toolbook ref. Chapter 23

24

MANAGING YOUR MANAGER

Let's face it, for most people sales is a peak-and-valley business. This is especially true for those people who rely strictly on commission to earn a living. It is vital that salespeople not slow down in the valleys, but that they trudge along steadily and earnestly, in order to make their way back to the peaks. Enforcing this strategy can separate a great Sales Manager from an average one. Motivate and coach your team during the low times just as fervently as you do during the good times. Encourage them to get back on a high as soon as possible, by keeping them charged up every single day.

Managing your Manager is about utilizing the strengths and tools that your Manager offers to help you with your journey. The trick to accomplishing this task is to share this information with our staff, and to encourage them to leave their ego on a shelf because they are going to have to ask for help. Therefore, the salespeople must also be able to manage the Manager, by getting the most help possible from that leader. They must be able to approach their supervisor on issues like:

- Lack of motivation
- Trouble recovering from rejection
- Assistance in closing techniques
- Feeling they can't win against the competition
- Feeling negatively-affected by incompetence of fellow staff
- Feeling unsure about their future with the company

Having sold everything from office furniture to film releases, I have seen and worked with my fair share of Sales Managers.

One of the best was Larry Rozumniak. He had the unique ability to meet with his sales team and say just the right things at the right times to positively affect the mindsets of his staff. Larry realized that people's attitudes could be turned around 180 degrees by one incident, one event or one conversation.

Take for example one of those indescribably low days spent at home in the middle of winter. Suddenly the phone rings, and your friend tells you he has just won a ski vacation and he is inviting you to join him. Fifteen minutes earlier you felt like a zero, now you feel like a hero! Your mood for the rest of the day has been altered with just one phone call. Larry used to be able to do that with me, I have done that with my staff, and hopefully you can do it with yours.

Not only should a Sales Manager say the right things, but he/she must also be able to *do* the right things. If one of your sales staff is having a rough day due to personal troubles, for instance, then consequently he's not doing very well on the sales floor. Is the best approach to send him home for the day? The caring Sales Manager might choose another tack and throw him a couple tickets to the next NHL game or a couple of passes to a good golf course for the afternoon. When you are lucky enough to employ good people, don't punish them for a bad day. Show them that they are valuable to you, and that you care enough to be patient with them through the odd difficult time. They are not producing in the mental state they're in anyway, and may be doing more harm than good by attempting to "stick it out".

A great Sales Manager is up to speed on his staff and the numbers they are producing, but sometimes numbers don't show it all. Let's say your top producer is unfailingly consistent for many years and then suddenly falters. The Manager can see that the numbers have been steadily dropping for a period of time, but how should he respond? Should the salesperson be fired? Absolutely not. This is a great opportunity for the Manager to take the time to find out what is going on with this person, and to explore possible methods of helping him out of his funk. Heck, maybe this is a perfect time to cross-train this individual and move him to another department for a fresh start.

The great Manager is also one who hires the kind of people who he knows are better than themselves. Unfortunately many Managers fear hiring people with seemingly limitless potential for fear of the safety of their own position. This is narrow, short-term thinking for a Manager. Remember, if you don't hire the best people, your competition will! Henry Ford was once bombarded with questions by a journalist/reporter who was hell-bent on belittling the automotive giant. Ford was asked intricate questions about the engineering, marketing, research and development of his company's product, but to the reporter's chagrin, he kept answering, "I don't know". The cocky journalist asked Ford how he could expect to effectively run his empire without possessing the knowledge to answer his questions. Ford replied that the answer was simple - all he needed to know was how to contact the high-level managers who ran each of his departments because *they* were the ones with the answers.

The same can be said about each of the organizations within which we all work. We must not be afraid to hire outstanding people and let them be the geniuses who provide *us* with all the right answers. Remember, when your employees shine, it makes you shine.

 Toolbook ref. Chapter 24

25

OUR MISSION IS ... AN ACRONYM

Great leaders make sure they share their company vision with all their employees. This is one of the reasons all companies should have a tight, well-constructed Mission Statement.

Does your company have a well-crafted Mission statement? Does it need one? Absolutely.

Whether your company has 5 or 500 employees, a Mission Statement is imperative to the unification of your staff. It is the best way to ensure that every single worker knows in what direction the company is heading. If your company has a Mission Statement, ask your employees if they can recite it by heart. You will likely find that many cannot.

Why is it important for an employee to know their company's mission? Simple, really! It's difficult to plan for every possible contingency in the course of a day's work; however, if your employees are familiar with the company's vision, they will be more likely to work towards achieving this objective regardless of the circumstance.

Experts have said there are numerous ways to remember things. Sometimes mere repetition works, some people "write lines". Some other people find that associating a picture with the words helps them to secure a phrase or thought. Whatever the case with your individual staff members, it is the Manager's job to help them find a way to learn and retain information which is important to their daily job functions. Let's use the company Mission Statement as a way to help foster and grow our memory skills.

Note: One of the best ways I have found to remember key principles is to put them in the form of an acronym. Our Mission Statement here at <u>Sales Meeting Companion</u> is:

"To educate Managers of Sales Teams by giving them the tools and techniques for putting on better Sales Meetings in order to better motivate and inform their employees."

We decided to break this wordy statement into an acronym which encompasses all its pertinent data within one word: TEAMS.

T oolbook to

E ducate

A nd

M otivate

S ales staff

'TEAMS' incorporates our mission statement and our company goal so that everyone will be able to remember our objectives by way of an acronym.

Franklin Covey, the parent company of the hugely successful Steven Covey book, "7 Habits of Highly Effective People", believes so strongly in Mission Statements that he displays on his web site reasons why every person should have their own personal Mission Statement. He says: "Creating a Personal Mission Statement will be, without question, one of the most powerful and significant things you will ever do to take leadership of your life. In it you will identify the first, most important roles, relationships, and things in your life - who you want to be, what you want to do, to whom and what you want to give your life, the principles you want to anchor your life to, the legacy you want to leave. All the goals and decisions you will make in the future will be based upon it. It's like deciding first which wall you want to lean your ladder of life against, and then beginning to climb. It will be a compass - a strong source of guidance amid the stormy seas and pressing, pulling currents of your life."

 Toolbook ref. Chapter 25

26

NEGOTIATION ... NEVER SAY NO

Many books have been written on negotiation, and one cannot begin to summarize all the pertinent points about this subject in one chapter. However, negotiation should entail two key principles. Number one, in order to make sure that you get the best possible deal, always be prepared to walk away. If you are not prepared to do this, then your astute customer will sense desperation and will milk your profit cow for all it's worth.

Number two, never say the word "no". The words "no" and "can't" are the devils of sales vocabulary and they should be exorcised from the tongues of our salespeople. Even if the customer is expecting unrealistic results from a transaction, we should always make a sincere effort to work within the parameters of their offer, with the addition of conditions of our own.

- "I want 20% off, I am familiar with kind of mark-up you apply."
- "Based on the size of this order, my head office requires terms of 6 months."

We should get into the habit of saying "yes" to our customers, and then entering into negotiations which include our own terms and conditions.

"Sure, no problem, what you're saying is that you like the _____, and now it's really only a matter of price shopping for you, in order to get the discount you are looking for. However, I'm sure you're aware that a business like ours doesn't operate successfully on such a low rate of profit - how could we do this and still manage to provide the customer service and support to which you are accustomed? How about _____, based on an order of _____? This way we both win!

We need to teach and instruct our staff to get themselves into the habit of erasing "no" and "can't" from their vocabularies.

Many people pay full retail price for a product or service with which they are thoroughly pleased. They love the product, the price, the packaging, the service, the salesperson - they're happy with everything! Inexperienced or just "weak" salespeople can too often find themselves falling into the "discount to build a client syndrome" Promote your products confidently and assume that people will pay full price because you are the best business to deal with. Many neophyte or desperate salespeople use this method (discounting) too often - this affliction should be constantly monitored and appropriately addressed when it becomes a rampant part of their selling style.

After we have gone over the features, functions and benefits of our product or service we should always ask for the order, at full price. Obviously this wouldn't work and isn't necessary for smaller ticket items. Smaller ticket items need only be displayed thoughtfully and priced appropriately within the marketplace. Larger ticket products and services are the ones that are more often subject to discounting.

Even large ticket items, though, have a significant audience in terms of people who need or want them, see the value in them, and are happy to pay full retail. In the automotive business I was trained to expect that a minimum of 20% of our clients would pay full list price for a vehicle. And this was in the car business, easily regarded as the business most likely to encounter heavy negotiating among its clientele! What percentage of people will pay full retail price in your industry? If you don't know, you should find out. Conduct your own study - call the manufacturer, call your competitors - come up with your own benchmark.

Most salespeople are on a commission or performance-based pay-plan so they are, counterproductively, affecting their own paychecks if they discount too much or too quickly. It is just too tempting, in our zeal to make a sale, to discount more than we should.

As Managers we should expand on *other* ways to ensure a sale today, by utilizing negotiating tools at our disposal, like:

- Terms
- Our price and value versus that of competing products
- Our resale value (if applicable)
- Volume discount if already applied to the price
- Dating (30, 60, 90, 120-day payment)
- Point of sale support
- Added value - something complimentary added in for a short time only
- Longer/better warranty and service maintenance
- Special finance rates

The list can go on and on.

During any negotiation we should formulate the bare minimum discount we can accept and try to get more than that. Shrewd negotiators add on extra items or extra amounts so that when "push comes to shove" they can remove them, thereby sweetening the deal to make it appear more valuable to the customer.

As much as it is not politically correct to say so, some cultures are much more prone to negotiate as a regular way of shopping than we are accustomed to in "Western Society". Within such cultures haggling and negotiating are a way of life, ingrained at an early age, and the outcome is that if such people do not "work a deal" then it is dishonorable to them and they will feel shamed if they did not at least try.

We can never tell who is going to "grind" us and who isn't, so we should always present our products at their full value and avoid the temptation to short-cut their value. If we diminish the sales process then we tend to shortchange the product's actual value when presenting it to our customer. If this happens, two things will result. One, we won't make the sale, because we have neglected to ensure the customer recognizes the product's full value. And two, if we do make a sale we won't get the potential full value that exists for that product.

Rules of Thumb:

- Present products and services fully
- Narrow down the products to the one that best suits the client's needs
- Describe features and benefits, disclosing examples that are relevant to your client's needs
- Create a sense of urgency and instigate mini-closes and trial closes throughout the transaction
- Cover any objections
- Close
- Cover any other objections
- Close the sale - write it up!

 Toolbook ref Chapter 26

27

HOPE

I believe "hope" to be is one of the most powerful words in the English language. Why? Simple really - when you've lost hope you've lost all potential. Hope keeps you hustling, moving, shaking, keeping the faith, and driving forward.

I asked my mentor, a very successful manager in the high-end stereo business, a question about what makes a great Manager or Leader. His response surprised me. "A great Manager is one who creates a safe, comfortable work environment for his or her employees, one in which they can set forth goals and make accomplishments in every aspect of their lives."

To support that statement: James Autrey and Stephen Mitchell, in their powerful business book, "Real Power", mention that "Good management is largely a matter of love, or if you're uncomfortable with that word, call it caring, because proper management involves caring for people, not manipulating them."

Let's face it, creating and achieving goals and giving people the tools with which to reach those goals is what enables all of us to succeed in life - not just at work. Certainly much of a person's mental well-being revolves around how good they are at their work, and what kind of difference they affect in their workplace. Accomplishing goals, long-range, mid-term, or short-term, all make us feel good once achieved.

Therefore, a Manager must be one who refreshes and renews hope within his/her employees anytime they feel let down by life. These same leadership qualities can, and should, be reflected to your customers by your staff.

Maybe the salesperson has to reassure the customer that the large order they are placing will be pulled through to their end user. "The way your business has been growing lately and considering the great staff with which you have surrounded yourself, this product will sell very well here." Or, "Look at you, Mr. Customer, I have dealt with you in the past and you are a straight-up person whom others look up to, you deserve this _____ for yourself and your family."

Directly or indirectly we are instilling hope in that customer. We are making them feel good about themselves. I know some of you may be reading this and thinking to yourself, "...what a bunch of bullshit we're feeding the customer in order to make them buy!"

Call it what you will, one thing for certain is that the most charming, charismatic people are those who consistently make others feel good about themselves. After all, charisma is, by definition, the transfer of enthusiasm to other people.

How do we transfer enthusiasm to others? By complimenting them in a sincere, forthright and timely manner, and by offering them hope when they need it.

Hope is extracted from us every night when we turn on the news or read the newspaper. It's high time we found a way to eschew this negativity and share a more positive feeling with our employees and customers.

Inevitably we are going to experience set-backs in the sales business. People are going to cancel orders, make excuses for not buying, buy from a competitor for a few dollars less, and neglect to make payments when they come due - and after we have put in an extraordinary amount of work. All these scenarios understandably create doubt in ourselves and our abilities.

If the customer senses doubt, you're finished. This is why we must exercise leadership in finding and illustrating what makes our employees special and valuable. Hopefully this kind of behavior will be contagious and rub off on our people, and they will go on to use it in every aspect of their lives.

 Toolbook ref. Chapter 27

PART III
TOOLBOOK

CONTENTS

Toolbook ref. Chapter 1

KNOW THE COMPETITION AND KNOW YOURSELF

In "The Art Of War", Sun Tzu suggests, "...Know the competition and know yourself and you will never lose in battle".
  "Insight gained from personal experience is ten times more valuable than instruction given by a manager or trainer".

This is why the Manager should implement a program in which the employees regularly visit the competition.

Prior to competitive shopping, what information does the employee need to have?

- Products sold
- Service policies
- Which competitive stores are the most successful?
- What products or services give us the most competition?

Arrange for select staff members to conduct competitive shopping surveys.

What observations were made?

1. Parking/ease of access
2. Good signage from the street/traffic
3. Greeting

4. Acknowledgement
5. Welcome
6. Ask you about your needs
7. Were they helpful throughout the whole transaction
8. Did they introduce themselves
9. Were they likeable, would you like to deal with them again?
10. Did they offer any other complementary items (upsells)?
11. Did they make it easy for you to buy - credit card, debit, check card?
12. Did they talk too much/too little/just right?
13. If you purchased, did they thank you for your business?
14. Friendliness level
15. Cleanliness level
16. Restroom visit and comments
17. What kind of signage did the store have helping you make a decision?
18. Did they explain to you the features and benefits of the products/services?
19. Were they able to answer your questions to your satisfaction?
20. Were they helpful?
21. Did they ask you open-ended questions?
22. Overall impression - *would you come back for future purchases?*

What features of the business did you consider to be outstanding?

_____

_____

What features did you find unpleasant, or even appalling?

_____

_____

Rate your competition like you are completing a Customer Satisfaction survey:

Excellent/Above average/Satisfactory/Substandard

*"There is nothing as convincing as a reality check from po-
tential buyers when trying to critique your own business and sales
staff."*

Mystery Shopping

*"The successful man is one who finds out what is wrong with
his business before his competitors do."*

What areas of the business are going to be critiqued?

Arrange for your business to be shopped. It is inexpensive - you
can often utilize students to do the work for a reasonable rate.

- Create a script for your mystery shopper to work with.
- List several questions that relate to your most popular products.
- Provide a response sheet on which the shopper can record
  accurate information.
- Include a space for their own personal comments and observations.
- Make sure you also mystery shop the competition for a direct comparison.

An example form for your mystery shopper could be:

1. Phone or visit the store and note the time the call or visit
   commenced.
2. Note whether the salesperson gave their name and a polite
   greeting.
3. Ask about a specific product that you have advertised as being on sale.
4. Was the salesperson aware of the sale?
5. Did they explain to you the main features of the item?

6. Did they make any effort to close the sale or ask for the business?
7. List overall impressions.
8. Personal observations and comments.

Toolbook ref. Chapter 2

EMPLOYEE INVOLVEMENT IN MEETINGS

"All key sales staff should get involved in sales meetings; whether they are facilitating parts of the meeting, discussing the pros and cons of the competition, or training the other staff."

Give the staff options as to how they would like to be involved in future meetings.

Decide what areas you would like to be involved in/responsible for in future meetings:

- Competitive shopping (results and evaluation)
- Training on new products or service
- Facilitate or chair the meeting
- Minutes recorder
- Devil's advocate
- Role playing

Review the results of the mystery shopping exercise:

Remember, mystery shopping should include a sample from your own store and several from your competitors. Review the results and keep the responses anonymous. Allow your staff to mull over the results and absorb their meaning.

- Discuss the positive aspects
- Discuss the negative or poor aspects
- Armed with this information, what positive changes can you make to your own sales presentation?

The successful employee/manager relationship hinges largely

on communications skills. We, as managers, must help foster and grow these skills within our staff. One great way to do this is to have individual staff members try their hand at running a sales meeting.

When staff members are asked to facilitate a meeting in place of their manager, what should they do?

Prepare:
- Meeting content
- Facilitator's notes
- Handouts
- Exhibits
- Advance memo
- Agenda
- Rehearsal of material
- Appointment of note-takers or minutes recorder

Discuss only problems with solutions that are within our control.

Toolbook ref. Chapter 3

KAIZEN

"All companies, regardless of size, should implement a KAIZEN policy."

Definition: Kaizen is continuous improvement and elimination of waste within the workplace.

Ways to improve through savings of:

- Time
- Manpower
- Staff turnover
- Energy costs
- Resources

Ways to eliminate waste through:

- Implementing a recycling program
- Improving organization
- Using time studies

Example: A factory worker realizes he can save time by not having to walk repeatedly to a different location to retrieve supplies if the supplies are re-located nearer his work station.

Can you list ways in which your company can improve or reduce waste?

_____

_____

_____

Have your sales staff list suggestions for improvements in their work place.

How can you implement systems or strategies that will allow these suggestions to be realized?

_____
_____
_____
_____

Example

(i) Have the employees write out what the problem is, and then what the possible solutions are
(ii) Have them now consider the costs to implement such a strategy and what the benefits would be : Cost/Benefit Analysis
Examples of costs

(a) manpower
(b) training needed
(c) energy consumed
(d) equipment needed
(e) other resources needed

MAKE IT EASY

"Reduce the stress level of your client by making it easy for them to find you, deal with you and buy from you."

Find ways to reduce your customer's stress:

First you must identify areas of potential stress in your business.

What aspects of your business make it stressful for the customer to purchase from you right now?

For example:

Multiple phone extensions, can't reach delivery personnel

How can we make it easier for the customer to remember us, get hold of us and purchase from us?

Consider tools like:

Customer files containing pertinent information. Sometimes you can include a photo of the customer (for later recognition) and tracking customer's buying habits to facilitate easier and friendlier transactions

Easily-accessed phone numbers, eg., magnetic business cards. Making your business easier to contact with both the web and your phone system (that should include voicemail and receptionist messaging

Making it easier for them to buy includes reducing redundant information collecting.

Providing a comfortable, no harassment environment.

Remember: Salespeople should become the expert for their customers by knowing the product as a consumer themselves (when practical). Encourage your staff to buy and use your products to facilitate their growth towards 'expert' status.

Toolbook ref. Chapter 5

QUESTIONING THE CUSTOMER

"Open ended questions will open the sales process. Closed questions will create a commitment and close the sale."

Open-Ended Questions

List examples of open-ended questions that are commonly used within our business.

_____

_____

_____

Closed questions are those which evoke yes or no answers.

When is the most important time to use this type of question?

_____

_____

_____

_____

Give examples of the best open-ended questions to use.

_____

_____

_____

_____

A closed question is used to evoke a short answer and bring a discussion to its conclusion. For example:

"Would you like to take delivery of your new car this week-end?"

Or "These items are selling fast should we set one aside for you?"

The answer is either yes or no. Use closed questions to create a commitment.

Toolbook ref. Chapter 6

CUSTOMER PERCEPTION IS REALITY

"The reality is, customers absorb everything from the first contact and a perception is then formed."

Airlines: Coffee ring stains give the impression that maintenance of aircraft is lacking.

Automobiles: Unclean engines after repair or maintenance give the impression that little or no work was performed on the vehicle.

Many impressions can be formed by the customer based on what they see, hear, feel and sense.

What are some aspects of our business that we can control in order to ensure that the customer perceives us in the right light?

Examples:

- Parking area
- Lobby
- Restrooms
- Packaging - dusty/unclean
- Our personal appearance
- Dress
- Sample merchandise

What can employees do to improve that first impression? Critique your sales area.

_____

_____

_____

_____

Toolbook ref. Chapter 7

BUILDING RELATIONSHIPS

"The best ways in which to build rapport with people are to find out if we share similar interests, hobbies, habits and activities."

<u>Demographics</u>	<u>Psychographics</u>
Age	Hobbies
Sex	Habits
Occupation	Lifestyle
Income	Interests
Marital status	Recreational activities
	Children's activities

Using the above examples, think of your best customers and list the psychographic reasons that you have a good rapport with them.

_____

_____

_____

_____

How can you develop this rapport-building policy to extend to more of your customers?

_____

_____

_____

_____

This information is especially helpful when selling to a personal customer base. Instruct your staff to make notes about a customer or potential customer as soon as possible after meeting them. These notes can be brief or elaborate. They should be organized and maintained.

If you are selling from business to other businesses, then knowing other critical data is important as well.

- How large is the company?
- How many employees in how many countries?
- How was the business started?
- Who is the principal operator - how did he/she get started?
- How has your contact in the business grown within the company?
- How many locations are there? Where?
- Other divisions?
- Is there a human-interest story within the company's rise/success?

PRESENTING MERCHANDISE

"Before we even open the doors, or open our mouths to talk, the customer is already formulating their purchase decision. Be aware of the importance of how merchandise is displayed and presented. Recognize the value of associating additional items that can be sold with the primary item."

List 3 of the top items that are sold, and list the potential complementary items that can be added on.

Principal   Secondary

_____

_____

_____

_____

What can we say and do when adding the secondary items that will give the initial or primary items more value?

_____

_____

_____

_____

Examples

- Most of our customers find that this _____makes the installation easier and quicker
- In order to protect and lengthen the lifespan of _____many of our customers get this as well.

- This_____would look spectacular with this, don't you think?

Toolbook ref. Chapter 9

MEET AND GREET

"Every employee, at every opportunity, should acknowledge, recognize and make guests feel welcome".

How should we greet our customers when we first meet them?

- Smile, be cheerful
- Welcome them
- Acknowledge all guests, even when they are dealing with others (can be just a nod or a Hello)

If we are "tied up" with another person when we see a client come in, what should we do?

- Acknowledge them
- Invite them to sit down, give them an idea how long you will be

Why and how do we do this?

The 'why' is easy: making customers feel welcomed and acknowledged is like making them part of the family - they will feel more comfortable about doing business with you and your company.

The 'how' just needs practice.

- Make a point to stop what you are doing even if just for an instant and say 'Hello'
- Adopt your own "ten-foot rule"
- Make eye contact and *SMILE*

Toolbook ref. Chapter 10

ENTERTAIN THEM

"The longer you can keep people in your place of business by entertaining them, the more likely they are to buy more of your product."

Do we want to entertain our clients?

Think of ways to keep our customers entertained.

- Comfortable environment and waiting area with TV
- Complimentary or sample items for your guests
- Children's recreation areas
- Compile work and product-related humorous stories for a notice board

What other ways can we entertain our customers while they are at our location?

MENTAL PREPARATION PREVENTS POOR PERFORMANCE

"Map out the sales transaction from greeting to goodbye, in order to maximize each opportunity."

Have your salespeople map out the strategy for their next cold call. (This should be broken down into three components.)

- The greeting
- The right questions and determination of needs
- Overcoming objections and asking for the order

_____
_____
_____
_____

Have your salespeople formulate a plan, on paper, for the second meeting with each individual customer.

_____
_____
_____
_____

Examples:
Opening ....(greeting and initial benefit statements)
Body ....(main reasons for buying)
Conclusion ....(how to achieve the desired result)

ADD CREDIBILITY TO WHAT YOU SAY

"Customers buy products they trust from people they trust."

It is important to build credibility with our customers.

- Know how trust is built.
- Remember that trust is almost always built over time.
- Remember that trust is built through honesty, even when this means you cannot recommend your own product.

What are ways in which to build trust and credibility with our customers?

- Upsell or downsell to find the appropriate product for an individual customer's needs
- Be prepared to provide third-party testimonials to reinforce and add credibility, for example:

  - Letters from existing or previous customers
  - Third-party material
  - Published trade or consumer articles
  - Information from other web sites
  - Reference letters from other companies

List ways in which you can add credibility to what YOU say.

_____

_____

_____

_____

Toolbook ref. Chapter 14

STAYING AHEAD OF YOUR CUSTOMER

"Do what you say you will do, keep your commitments, and inform your customer ahead of time if there are any changes to their expectations."

What does staying ahead of your customer mean to you?

- Be true to your word, even when – *especially when* - it means you have to admit an error on your part.
- Let them know *as soon as you know* about any changes to their initial product or service expectations. Under-promise and over-deliver. Allow a time cushion with delivery dates or completion times.

_____

_____

_____

Think of a time in the recent past when we failed to stay ahead of our customer - what happened?

_____

_____

_____

_____

Think of a time in the recent past when we *did* stay ahead of our customer - what happened?

_____

_____

_____

_____

How can we use examples of our failures to improve our performance in this area in future?

_____

_____

_____

_____

Toolbook ref. Chapter 15

TAKE CONTROL

"Put your customer in the driver's seat, and keep yourself on the road ahead of them, showing them the way to go."

Is having control important during the selling process? How?

_____

_____

_____

_____

What are some ways in which we can take control of the customer in our business?

1. Make sure not to skip any part of the sales process.
2. Once a selection is made, review all its benefits.
3. Control the conversation - use open-ended questions.
4. Ask the customer the right questions, and never talk too much.
5. Remember the old adage, "telling and not selling".
6. When the customer is slow to make a selection, be politely assertive by introducing another choice.
7. Make sure to pinpoint the decision maker - ask if there is another person involved in the decision-making process.
8. Provide a demonstration without having been asked.
9. At the appropriate time, use closed questions to obtain the commitment.

What are some ways in which we can lose control during the selling process?

- Not being assertive at the right time.
- Using unprofessional language or "off color" humor.
- Using disparaging remarks about another person/business in order to make yourself look better.
- Disclosing the final price before you have had an opportunity to review all the benefits, and how they relate to saving the customer money.

Toolbook ref. Chapter 16

RULE OF THREE

"Providing information, making a point, and achieving a strong positive impression in your customer's mind will improve exponentially when you invoke the Rule of Three."

Did you ever stop to wonder why so many things are offered in THREES? Here are the top three reasons:

1. It's easy to remember any directory of items which appears in sequences of three. Eg., area codes, social insurance numbers (Canada and U.K.), bank account numbers.
2. Simplification - sometimes the more choices one is given, the more opportunity there is for confusion.
3. Three is just right - any more than three choices is often too much information; any less than three is not credible enough.

List the main products/services your company sells.

_____
_____
_____
_____

List three major benefits for each item that is offered:

_____

1.
2.
3.

1.
2.
3.

1.
2.
3.

1.
2.
3.

List three reasons for your customer to buy right now/today:

1.
2.
3.

Toolbook ref. Chapter 17

MAKE A NOTE

"As soon as possible following every transaction or conversation with a customer, the salesperson should record the pertinent details of the discussion. Include notes about the customer and the topics discussed."

What are some points to record after you meet a customer?

- Client concerns
- Their company's needs
- Client interests
- Personal data (vacation destinations, family, hobbies, etc.)
- Company's achievements
- Client's personal achievements

_____
_____
_____
_____

Which are the most important aspects to remember?

How could we include these items in our next conversation with our customer?

_____
_____
_____
_____

Toolbook ref. Chapter 18

UNIQUENESS

"Sales meetings should regularly include highlighting your company's particular strengths and unique qualities, including how they compare with those of your competition."

Have every salesperson come up with their own reasons describing unique features of your company. The manager can collect everyone's answers and create a master list for the staff to read and discuss. This list could be written out on an overhead or a whiteboard, or be made into a PowerPoint presentation. In this way you will likely find that together, the staff will come up with more positive reasons to promote their business than you could have accomplished on your own.

Here are some examples of sub-topics which may be helpful to you in your efforts to facilitate a worthwhile group discussion.

What aspects of our business are unique compared to those of our competitors?

Store

- Hours of operation
- Years in business
- Location(s)
- Parking/ease of access
- Our history of good relations with the manufacturer

Service

- What we do better
- What we do quicker/faster

- How we package
- Return policies
- Customer support staff; 1-800 assistance, etc.
- Information packets we provide with our product
- Our installers/technicians

Team /Personnel/Manpower

- Outstanding performers
- Outstanding receptionist
- Great problem-solvers
- Super management
- Exemplary shippers/receivers
- Research and Development

Toolbook ref. Chapter 19

FOLLOW-UP

"Consistent follow- up is the difference between an average sales-person and superstar salesperson."

There are two types of follow- up, one occurs before the sale has taken place, and the second occurs after the sale has been made.

When you perform follow-up, it is always good to have something new to provide your prospect. It doesn't have to be something huge, but there should be some new information that you can pass on to them, along with your confirmation of what has taken place.

Pre-follow-up should entail what?

It could be that you offer:

- Different finance rates
- Improved features
- Improved availability
- More attractive terms, etc.

After-sales follow-up should happen when and how often?

_____

_____

_____

Toolbook ref. Chapter 20

HOW TO HANDLE OBJECTIONS

"Objections raised by your customer should be welcomed as opportunities to respond positively and strengthen your sales pitch."

List the top three products that your company sells, and underneath list the most common objections that are heard in relation to each item.

Product A.

_____

_____

_____

Product B.

_____

_____

_____

Product C.

_____

_____

_____

A successful method for countering objections is also based on the Rule of Three:

Cushion – Rephrase – Solution

- Cushion the objection by using an empathetic statement to show your concern and understanding.

- Rephrase the objection by repeating it back to the customer in a different way.
- Provide a solution to the concern by pointing out a positive feature that will overcome the concern or explain a misunderstanding.

THE SELECTION PROCESS

"Qualifying the customer, assessing their needs, and making a selection are crucial components to making the sale."

What questions could we ask our customer that will enable us to narrow down the selection process?

_____

_____

_____

_____

_____

_____

There should be a limit to how many choices we offer. Remember, offering too many choices will invariably confuse the customer. ("More is More" complex.)

Should we limit the number of choices we offer a customer? Why?

_____

_____

_____

_____

_____

Most people do not want to be pioneers with the products or services they buy, they prefer to know they are buying a tried and true favorite. So how can we illustrate this to a customer? What kind of terminology could we use?

_____

_____

_____

_____

Examples

1. Many of our customers _____

2. Our best customers choose _____

3. This is our best-selling _____

List a few more and put them in a context that relates to your business.

_____

_____

_____

_____

_____

Toolbook ref. Chapter 22

TELEPHONE FUNDAMENTALS

"The telephone can be your best friend or your worst enemy. Ensure it is employed to its maximum advantage within your business."

How should your company greeting go?

Break it into three major components:

- Greeting
- Identify yourself
- Department

_____

_____

_____

_____

What are some potential problems which can arise during the telephone process?

1. Neglecting to ask for the order
2. Not taking enough control
3. Not setting up an appointment
4. Not getting the customer's name and other pertinent information
5. Not thanking the customer

Additional possible telephone problems:

- It takes too long to be answered (a goal should be to pick it up on the first ring)
- Messages are not passed on to intended recipient
- Customers can't get through to a 'live' body (voicemail is part of our lives and it can be great, but in many situations your clients need to speak to a person, not a machine)
- Neglecting to ask for the order
- Neglecting to set up a firm appointment
- Not having enough control (neglecting to get the customer's name, phone number, and other pertinent data)
- Not building enough rapport
- Not elaborating on the strengths of the company, instead focusing on price and price alone
- Neglecting to thank the customer for their call and their patronage

Call your own business and record your concerns and ways in which they can be remedied.

....
....
....
....
....

Toolbook ref. Chapter 23

COFFEE CLUB

"Successful people make a habit of doing things which unsuccessful people do not do." - Joe Girard, Superstar Car Salesman, speaking about those salespeople who sit around in groups discussing sports, the weather and other time-wasting topics - when instead they could be out there drumming up business for themselves.

What do the Coffee Clubbers do within your organization?

....

....

....

....

What can we do during the non-peak times to help generate more business?

- Prepare sales kits
- Make phone calls and try to generate business
- Re-visit or re-connect with past clients via mail, email, or phone
- Follow up with unsold prospects
- Contact leads found on the company web site
- Search out new leads through directories at the library, e.g., like: wwwinfousa.com and www.infocanada.ca
- directory, New Home listings, new businesses licensed with the city

What more can we do during slow times to better prepare ourselves for when we are busy?

- Research the competition
- Phone-shop the competition
- Read and keep up-to-date on trade journals
- Expand your network of people by looking into and possibly joining different groups, associations and clubs

Toolbook ref. Chapter 24

MANAGE YOUR MANAGER

"As Managers, we must be able to illustrate to our staff that we are there to help, but that ultimately they are steering their own ship and they must be pro-active in seeking assistance in their jobs."

In what ways can the staff enlist the help of the management?

- Come up with realistic forecasts and projections
- Create ways to meet these projections
- Get re-motivated
- Get training on new products
- Role-play to sharpen sales techniques
- Work to improve organizational techniques

Are there internal issues which need to be discussed in order to make the sales process easier and more productive? Are there personality conflicts within the sales team?

Which types of motivation most impact you?

- Recognition
- Praise
- Money
- Gifts for your family
- Promotions

- Company sports tickets
- Use of goods sold

Toolbook ref. Chapter 25

OUR MISSION IS ... AN ACRONYM

Experts have said there are numerous helpful ways to remember something, and one of the best ways is to break it down into the form of an acronym."

What is your company's Mission Statement?

_____

_____

_____

_____

Does your company have a Vision Statement? What is it?

_____

_____

_____

_____

_____

_____

Can we break this down into an acronym using all the key words?

_____

_____

_____

_____

What other list or hard-to-remember vital piece of information can we simplify with an acronym?

_____

_____

_____

_____

_____

_____

_____

_____

Toolbook ref. Chapter 26

NEGOTIATION MEANS ....NEVER SAY NO

"There are many aspects of negotiation which can be taught and learned; however, we find that two in particular ring truest for our purpose here. One is, 'Try to give the impression that you could walk away from any deal'. Two, although this sounds contrary to the first rule, is, 'Try to eliminate "no" and "can't" from your vocabulary during sales transactions'".

We should always present our products and benefits as though doing so for the first time. By leaving out vital information just because we already know it all, we are jeopardizing our best chance for a sale, as well as opening up the situation to customers who practice "grinding".

If the customer is asking for a discount or special terms/rates which are unacceptable to us, how should we respond?

_____
_____
_____
_____
_____

Without saying "no" or "can't", how can we respond to the customer?

Examples:

- Not a problem, you will have to secure an order of this many to get that rate.
- Sure we can, however, our conditions include...

- Yes, but in order to do that you will also need to order ____ _____ at this price.

Toolbook ref. Chapter 27

INSTILLING HOPE

"There are few words in the English language that hold as much power as the word 'hope'. As salespeople we are certain to experience ups and downs, but it is important in our business to always be able to convey hope in our own actions as well as in the mindsets of our customers."

What things should we be hopeful of?

_____

_____

_____

_____

How can we instill hope to our customers?
(nonverbal)

_____

_____

_____

(verbal)

_____

_____

_____

Think about helping our employees to set and achieve their goals - on daily, weekly, monthly, and yearly basis.

How do we instill hope in our employees?

Compliment them on their strengths and verify to them their value within the organization.

INDEX

ACKNOWLEDGEMENTS

A NOTE OF APPRECIATION

The authors would like to thank:

Our Editor…. Eva Marie Valdes

Our friend…..Dave Turnbull

RECOMMENDED FURTHER STUDY, TRAINING AND REFERENCE

Rocky Mountain Managers Summit

We invite the reader to engage in a three day Manager's workshop that will recharge, rejuvenate and educate leaders. Held in the spectacular Canadian Rockies, these seminars include internationally renowned guest speakers, an opportunity to mix with sales leaders from other industries and workshops designed to help you focus on achieving your personal maximum. Space is limited, so act now to take part in a once-in-a-lifetime opportunity to attend.

The Authors will be available for Staff training, Company evaluations, Keynote presentations, Conferences and Workshops. Please send your comments and requests to salesmc@telus.net

We will be sure to contact you promptly.

Email us or visit our website at www.companionlearning.com for more information.

Thank you for your interest in Sales Meeting Companion.

Dave and Mike

Suggested reading and study

"How to Win Friends and Influence People" by Dale Carnegie

"Managing Through People" by Dale Carnegie and Associates, Inc.

Enrol in a Dale Carnegie Leadership course
www.dalecarnegie.com

"Mastering Your Way To the Top" by Joe Girard
www.joegirard.com

Join: Toastmasters International
www.toastmasters.org

"Customers For Life" by Carl Sewell

"The One Minute Manager Builds High Performing Teams"
by Ken Blanchard, Eunice Parisi-Carew
www.kenblanchard.com

"Top Performance" by Zig Ziglar
www.zigziglar.com/Ziglar/books.do

"Making Your Dreams come True" by Marcia Weider

"Real Power" by Mitchell and Autrey

"Rich Dad, Poor Dad" by Robert T. Kiyosaki

"The Power of Focus" by Jack Canfield, Mark Victor Hansen, Les Hewitt

ISBN 1412028558